WAYS YOUTH LEARN

I Am the Dream Power of Youth[1]

I am one with the mysterious drive, buried within the inner
    essence of every living thing,
That urges it on from what-it-is to the unknown land of
    what-it-is-to-be.

The explosive power in the simplest cell,
The force that guides the stars,
The inner urge that moves in all living things,
The influence that takes men out of caves and scatters them as
    pioneers throughout the world,
The stimulus of revolutions,
The soul of the search for truth,
The mainspring of national life,
The initial essence of the arts,
The impulse that lies at the root of all efforts toward religion—

These, and I, are the plan of the creative God for bringing
    to light the outlines of His will.

He hid us in the heart of things that, by the self-activity of
    His universe, that will should someday be revealed.

WAYS
YOUTH
LEARN

CLARICE M. BOWMAN

HARPER & BROTHERS, PUBLISHERS

New York

TO MY MOTHER

Mrs. Willie Frances Bowman

whose life gives beauty

and a wealth of meaning

to the word

"teacher"

Library of Congress catalog card number: 52-8462

CONTENTS

ACKNOWLEDGMENTS

Continuing gratitude is expressed:

To all who have taught, and are now teaching me . . .
"For rigorous teachers seized my youth,
And purged its faith, and trimm'd its fire,
Showed me the high, white star of Truth,
There bade me gaze, and there aspire." (Matthew Arnold)

To "friends of youth" (their teachers, counselors, parents, pastors, camp leaders, others) with whom I have been privileged to associate in travels over America these fourteen years. It is they who have written this book in truth, through the ideas they have suggested, the problems they have raised, the insights they have shared, and the buoyant belief in youth and in youth's God to which their lives have witnessed.

To young people I have known . . . and others I hope to know.

To my fellow staff members of the Methodist Board of Education, Division of the Local Church, Department of Youth Work—for the impact of their powerful minds, the "good salt" of their helpful criticism, the "swell fun" of their companionship, and the prodding challenge of their committed lives.

To the publishers and authors granting permission to use quotations included in this work.

To the Bradley Williams family in whose home I sojourned while doing some work on the manuscript, and whose courageous Christian churchmanship challenges; and to Margueritte, delightful guinea pig.

To Miss Anne Stroh, former secretary and lifetime friend, whose keen mind and social conscience awaken and inspire, and whose interest in this work has helped keep my shoulder to the plow.

To my Father and Mother, my first and most esteemed "teachers."

INTRODUCTION

Well might this book be called "adolescent" itself. Its gestation and growth over the past fourteen years coincides with the life span of many "teenagers" today. And even now, while it is being assigned to paper, it cries out, "Unfinished!" More ideas to be discovered. Better methods to be tried out. New frontiers for search and research. The very subject matter of this book is adventurous. For whenever any group of energetic young persons and adult friends get together, something new is about to happen on the face of the earth—for better or for worse.

Let the reader (shall we say user?) of this material here regard it —not as a monument over the grave of static principles and methods —but rather as a trumpet call to "greater things than these shall ye do!"

The adult churchman interested sufficiently in young people to pick up this book will call to mind firsthand experiences he has had, or is having, with these clear-eyed, quick-thinking, dynamic individuals somewhere between the ages of twelve and twenty-four. They will march across the center stage of his thinking as he surveys the suggestions in this book. Upon his own firsthand ideas and his loving Christian concern for these youth, let him build his convictions as to what teaching means—from the adult's angle; and what learning means—from the young person's angle. No book can *tell* teachers how to teach or youth how to learn. Printed pages can but suggest some leads. The reader is urged most cordially to carry on two-way conversation with the author all the while. As with recipes, methods must be taken off paper and translated into actualities with real groups of young people in a real world. Not all methods suggestions will be found to "work." An idea for an activity of learning

7

may touch off a spark in one group, and fail to catch hold at all in another. The same method may elicit a totally different response in the same group at two different periods of time. There is nothing static, nothing foolproof, nothing magical about methods.

But methods do *matter*. For they have to do with the stuff of life. They are like Peter's keys to the kingdom. Good or poor teaching methods can unlock doors, leave doors closed, or even lock doors for young persons in their thinking, deciding, praying, living. Who knows the number of young lives who have been lost eventually to the Christian way because of poor teaching and poor teachers in home and church? An intermediate may "draw silly pictures in the back of the hymnbook or the Bible" or he may "etch their lessons upon his heart," depending upon the kind of adult friend he had to work with him as "teacher" in that Sunday school class or evening fellowship meeting. It makes a difference what we teach and *how* we teach it. Surely our Christian faith is worth our utmost in craftsmanship as good teachers! Some may express impatience with materials on methods as if they were an inconsequential, take-it-or-leave-it matter. But method and message go together. Poor methods may get in the way of a young person's response to the Christian message. Some may minimize techniques as ephemeral and unrelated to the timeless truths of religion. But the best we know about good methods traces back for its clues to the *way* the Great Teacher taught as well as to what He said.

But frankly, the concern of this book is for more than methods: it is for a burning sense of mission—*Christian evangelical mission*—in the hearts of all adults who would work with youth in home and church today: for a consciousness of calling, of divine partnership, of dangerous alternatives, of split-second urgency "shivering throughout him" (using the image in F. W. H. Myers' poem about St. Paul). To teach young people today is evangelism—or rather, *can* be. There is an "if" and it is dead serious. That "if" is threefold: it asks about the *quality of life* the teacher leads—whether his essential witness is affirmatively for the Christian way, or palely neutral, or even against; second, it asks about the *message* the teacher has to impart—whether it rings with the authenticity of firsthand personal experience or not;

8

and third, it asks about his *methods*—whether they be the kind that will attract and appeal to youth, amidst vortexes of other conflicting calls today.

A prayerful purpose of this book, therefore, is to frighten teachers of young people. If some, overpersuaded in the first place to take a class or meet with an evening session, feel they lack sufficient Christian commitment and are frightened away from teaching until they can make such commitment—good! Others may go to their knees, as many workers with youth throughout the land are doing these days, in fresh consecration and renewal of purpose. Rising from their knees, they will seek out eagerly such training class, workers' conference meetings, books and other helps as will aid them in deepening their insights and sharpening their skills. Opportunities of this sort are to be found in abundance. Denominational and interdenominational headquarters will be glad to supply information. Helpful courses can be secured through correspondence. Reading lists will be furnished. With the regular curriculum units appearing in denominational periodicals are exceedingly practical and helpful teachers' and counselors' suggestions. No one need lack for guidance. But the important thing is that his heart be warmed; that he be baptized with a sense of mission about his task of guiding youth in home and church in a day like this . . . for youth's own sake, yes; for the church's sake and for the sake of the church of tomorrow, yes; but particularly for the sake of the purposes of the Living God.

For whom is this book prepared? For anyone interested in young persons and eager that they find and follow the Christian way. That means perhaps almost every churchman not in the youth age range himself! But primarily, this material is offered those in positions to influence young people particularly: their first and foremost "teachers" in the home, their parents; their counselors, teachers and advisers in the church (including pastors especially); other workers with these same young persons in related character-building agencies —in short, this material is offered any "intentional" teachers of youth, those who, as Dr. Paul H. Vieth has defined, are their "friends with a purpose."

The locus of this book is *the local church*. Thither come on a

Sunday morning or evening or weekday, bunches of boys and girls 12-14 years, somewhat taller bunches of young folks of senior high years, 15-17, and still taller and more mature youth of college and career ages, 18-23. From this local church go out influences into home and community and larger world. It has been felt that Sunday school teachers and those meeting with young people in Sunday evening fellowship meetings and related activities needed some helps directed to their "regular" week-by-week contacts, their use of printed helps, their use of Bible, guidance of youth participation and worship.

No attempt is made here to deal with the complex problem of weekday religious education administratively, although it is hoped that persons teaching in weekday systems may discover helps on methods, and on relation of what they are doing to the church program with youth.

Nor is there attempted here a complete picture of the "youth program" as it obtains in many denominations, with its maze of organizational structuring and beyond-the-local-church activities. The chosen focus is rather upon what happens in a little Sunday school class or a committee or evening meeting of young people in a small or medium or large church. Here we believe is found the heartbeat of church work with youth, the very heartbeat of the Christian religion. With what dynamics is this group discussion fraught? What is the adult's role? What ways will youth share in planning? Will what is thought or decided or done here cast its weight on the side of Christian progress or no? The mere fact that said class or meeting is under the auspices of the church is no guarantee of the answer. He who calls himself "teacher" in the situation holds the key.

A certain grave danger attends any book on teaching methods: danger that it may cause teachers to focus attention upon *themselves* (What are my characteristics as a teacher? How well am I doing?). Rather, the point of view with which a worker approaches this book, and his continuing task is that of *upreach* Godward, and *outreach* youthward. Let not himself as teacher command the center of his attention. He is but "prompter from the wings," while youth themselves play their part upstage. Someone has described a good teacher
10

as one who leads young people to a door, and then steps aside himself so as not to be in their way when they enter for themselves.

While the introductory parts of this book may sound pessimistic, its general note is that of boundless faith in the power of the Christian gospel to triumph even in a world like this; boundless faith in young people and in "that of God" that is ever working within them long before we their humble teachers come upon the scene (and often works its good work in spite of what we do or say); boundless faith in teachers of youth in home and church and otherwhere as they grow in their commitment and skills; and boundless faith in what can happen for the Kingdom of God when "youth and their teachers together" seek to make Jesus' way their way.

CLARICE M. BOWMAN

I

TEEN YEARS TODAY

Behold, I have set before thee this day, Life . . . and death.
DEUTERONOMY 30:15

We are living in a "grand and awful time." Every hour brings lightning changes. Men and nations face decisions that will be for time and for eternity. Our lifetimes have seen greater changes than two hundred years before, or two thousand years before that. Civilization has been a long time coming to the boiling point, but we are now caught up in the boiling. One finds it hard these days to escape the feeling that he is but a pawn in the grip of titanic forces; hard to keep his perspectives straight; hard not to echo the Psalmist of old, "I am troubled; I am bowed down greatly; I go mourning all the day long." For over the hills of time comes again the hollow call that startled the children of Israel in their day of decision: "This day, O man, have I set before thee life and death."

—*Death?* So serious as all that? Pervasive death in the physical realm—yes, a possibility. Once more the alarming word pictures of judgment day flicker on the horizons of our imaginations. But death deeper than the physical! For *unless* those who are now young learn how to practice democracy as a way of life and not merely a word; *unless* those who are now young find fellowship with God and make the way of His Son their way—the "hopes and fears of all the years" may go down with those now living . . .

These who are now young people had no choice about being born to live in such an hour of destiny. But because they are youth now, they are earmarked for greatness.

Growing Up in an Anxious Age[1]

Growing up has always had its stresses and strains. No doubt each younger generation from the beginning of time has had its own

13

questions to face—questions relating largely to growing as a self and finding one's way in the world of people and things. In earlier times, adolescents busy with their own personal insecurities had some degree of stability to count on in the world about them. But security is what this generation does not have—not in their homes, not in their social relationships, not in the international scene, not in their future dreams.

Fear has won a beachhead. People seem to be awaiting some nameless catastrophe. Dark shadows of grief caused by war tragedies are still felt in many homes. Millions of the fittest in the youth generations just before them have been slaughtered. Uncounted thousands surviving are enfeebled, their health and strength undermined by disease or injury.

Broken homes break young lives. With no warm strong family affection to fall back upon, they drift farther and farther—not only from the home base, but from what home used to stand for. As always, beer halls and worse places are ready to coin shekels from wandering youth. And the wanderers are getting younger. The narcotics vender does not ask about age.

These are not "problem youth" but youth *with* problems, many of which have been thrust upon them as innocent victims. They have a world to grow up in today, seething in the aftermath of wars, writhing in tensions, groveling in insecurities. Old and outmoded political structures try desperately to survive as new structures struggle in the throes of coming to birth. Youth's world is plagued by economic contradictions and baffled by propaganda.

Adults may pause, however, to reflect that for youth this type of world is "normal." They have no other norms by which to judge, as have those who are older and who have known different times. Youth take "modern" inventions and standards of living for granted, which to older persons appear somewhat marvelous. The world of jet propulsion, fruit for breakfast, television, and interplanetary travel seems as familiar and nonextraordinary to youth as an old shoe.

Community, national, and world forces impinging particularly upon young lives today include:

1. Disruption of family units; increased transiency; increased number of divorces; lowered moral idealism.
2. Interruption of youth's usual patterns for life-planning; difficulties as to education, vocation, marriage, and finding a place to live.
3. Economic contradictions: abnormal boom times with money cheap, and purchasing "hogwild"; then unemployment, fear of inflation and depression; growing popularity of get-money-the-easy-way ideas: jackpots, contests, gambling.
4. Accentuation of the sex problem: lowered sex standards; elimination of the external restraints of fear of social disease and fear of pregnancy; returning military personnel with lowered standards; lack of home training; unrestraint in high school crowds.
5. Frustrations, particularly among boys: getting "steamed up for great adventure" but facing ordinariness; hoodlumism on upsurge.
6. Increase in racial and social tensions.
7. Confusion as to ethical standards.
8. Drink rampant—even making inroads among names on church rolls; widespread and psychologically subtle propaganda encouraging drinking; frank promotion through mass communications. Increasing use of narcotics.
9. The world continuously apprehensive over the possible outbreak of its worst war.[2]

Young people cannot help knowing that whole populations on the earth's surface but barely survive, groping in pitiable hunger through cheerless days. They suspect that something is dreadfully wrong in national and international planning.

John is twelve years old. He is in the seventh grade. He has been working for a week on a composition entitled, "Civilization." It was a baffling assignment for John but finally he finished it. When he turned it in to the teacher, he attached a note to it.

"Dear Teacher:

"I have made twelve different rough copies of this composition and each time it comes out different. This is the best I can do with civilization. I am sorry about it. Yours truly, John."

This is what John had to say about civilization:

"Civilization is all around us. It is what all of your years on earth add up to and it is mostly wars and fights of one kind or another. If countries aren't doing it people are. Like my mother and father. Last month they finally got a divorce and now I haven't got a father any more. Instead of letting my father club my mother like cavemen did civilization gives them divorces. This is all I have to say about civilization except that I think wars and fights are not especially good for people and the older civilization gets the harder it is to know who to like and who to hate."[3]

Jet Planes and Moral Judgments

We can manufacture jet planes, we can turn out Diesel engines at will, we have the secret of the atom bomb; but given the situation of a boy or girl of dubious reputation, we have no secret formula nor any assured know-how for changing bad character into good character. Neither do we know how to uncover moral leadership—the leadership of individuals of stable character with ability to "conceive a moral principle, accept it as right, and to defend it when the moral judgments of the community seem to violate it." Here are areas for research . . .[4]

What shall Judy take as "right"—what her grandmother says, what she sees glamorized in movies or television, what the gang does, what her parents insist upon, or what the church teaches? No longer are definite, clean-cut standards of morality supported in American communities generally. Many of the older codes are cracking. "Do what you can get by with" seems to be a rule exemplified in some of the lives of adults around town. Cheating, once a rarity in schools, is more and more an accepted practice. The principal of a small high school requested parents to decide what should be the school's attitude on the question of smoking in the rooms; the parents were unable to reach a majority decision. No wonder young people find it difficult to know what to do or not to do.

On many questions, they note in adults actions out of harmony with their words. Taught one set of convictions in peacetime, and a totally different set during war, they wonder if the church—if anybody—has a message that can be depended upon.

Veteran pilots of nineteen years, after handling powerful planes

16

with Superman efficiency, rebel at being treated "like little kids" by home, school, place of employment, government. Notable dramas depict the return of the Negro soldier to a democracy not yet ready for him. Millions taught fierce skills of killing and imbued with attitudes to match those skills find adjustment to tame, complacent community life difficult. Hordes of younger youth, intermittently employed perhaps at prematurely large salaries, turn to gangsterism for adventure and quick money. Craving adventure and willing to manufacture it at utmost danger to themselves, they get their hot rods "souped up" and speed through games on the highways to teenicide. Courage, imagination, skill and daring, not harnessed to worthy goals, end up in a mass of twisted steel and mangled bodies on the road at four in the morning.

Unresolved problems shake and often split asunder young personalities. Doctors cannot be trained fast enough to keep up with the needs. Besides those labeled "patients" are thousands who grow up to become society's problems rather than its problem solvers.

Does twelve-year-old Johnny learn from the comic book to put an over-inflated value on physical power to the exclusion of spiritual power? Does the radio's lowest common denominator approach to entertainment account for the reluctance of a senior group to use imagination and ingenuity in planning a banquet program? Do radio comedians encourage among youth sensitivity to the subtle and genial forms of humor—as distinguished from the gag and the slapstick? Where are young people picking up their standards of taste? What do they identify as mediocre? vulgar? banal? worthful? abiding? uplifting? What has brought Bill and Joe so near to the thin edge of crime?[5]

What is the over-all impression young people get from the community life around them as to what would be a desirable "way of life?" Do the influences playing upon them bid them to weigh issues and decide carefully and prayerfully, or is there sensation mongering that would sway the millions (and to the extent that this latter seeps in, what is it but the brewing of dictatorships)?

Youth are being taught by the community's attitude to the church. How is the church regarded by those a young person knows best —As a worthy institution, yes . . . but one a fellow can take

17

or leave? Are church services and church work regarded as of high significance, deserving of a place of priority among priorities like football practice, band, glee clubs, drama groups, social affairs, and such like?

Even more seriously, community forces influence youth's regard for religion itself. "For the aged, the sick, and the women," perhaps . . . Or, "Religion is okay in its place, but best not get hot and bothered; people will think you fanatic." Or, "There will be plenty of time to think about such things when I'm older and sit by the fire." "Let the preacher steer clear of controversial issues like race and stick to his Bible." "Religion is against the things you enjoy most doing." The attitudes church people spread abroad help create the community attitude; help determine whether in *that* community the church stands fearlessly for Jesus' teachings regardless of politics or pressures; help determine whether in *that* community religion is regarded as a matter of rosy-glow emotional feeling in comfortable, comforting services or a prod to decisive thinking and courageous action against evils thwarting the realization of a kingdom of love.

Secularism is teaching youth: people's preoccupation with money, and the things money can buy; people's living as if this life were all and religion a quaint custom of bygone days; people's moving through their days and years *as if there were no God!* Little wonder that some are moved to lament that we have entered a "post-Christian" era.[6] "Christianity's major rival in the western world," thinks Georgia Harkness, "is secularism."[7]

The Christian gospel receives its most devastating blows, often unconsciously, from those who stand within a long Christian inheritance but who now pass it by in preoccupation with much that seems more exciting.[8]

What, then, is secularism? It is the ordering and conducting of life as if God did not exist; it is the placing of hedonistic and cultural goals above and in place of those of the Kingdom; it is deference to the methods and products of science to the depreciation of all other truth and all other values. . . . Secularism is characterized, not universally but in startlingly large areas of modern life, by a superficial optimism and inner despair.[9]

Secularism has almost wholly engulfed our culture and is on the way

18

to swallowing up our churches and our souls. We no longer live in "the Christian West," but in a mission field ripe for harvest. The seed of the gospel, though sown on rocky and thorny ground, still has a chance by the power of God to bring forth fruit for our redemption. By the outcome of such sowing the earthly and eternal destinies of men will be determined.[10]

The issue is laid squarely at the doorstep of the little white country chapel, or the red-brick church on the edge of town, or the high-spired temple at a swirling city intersection. Will this church be able first of all, in a time when churches are losing youth while enrollment of other ages soars to an all-time high, to reach and hold its young people? What will be the quality of Christian guidance this church offers these young who are now "old enough to make permanent decisions yet young enough to make radical changes?" What *teachers* will this church offer its youth? *What* will they teach? *How* will they teach?

II

CHRISTIAN AFFIRMATIONS
AND YOUTH WORK

In holiness and righteousness before him, all the days of our life.   LUKE 1:75

What does the church say to young people growing up in an anxious age?

It affirms that persons can be helped to grow toward God, that the influence of Christian home life is immeasurably powerful; that, in addition, certain activities can be set up by the church itself through which children, youth, and adults can be helped to know more clearly what following Jesus means, and to translate that knowledge into all of living—personal and social.

Foundational to the church's program of Christian education is the belief that every child can—

Start early on a path which will lead to worthy membership in the church and in the family of God;

Learn to take God into account, to love Him, trust Him, thank Him, serve Him;

Learn ways of love, friendship, gentleness, peace, helpfulness, and Christian discipleship;

Begin to formulate Christlike ideals and purposes centering not in self and comfort, ease and possessions, but in fellowship with God and others who make up God's family on earth.

That these goals may to some extent be achieved, the church provides adult leaders who will work with children of the different ages; rooms and equipment; a time schedule; money; lesson materials; helps for parents, and encouragement to them in their role as teachers of religion; training for the workers in both home and church.

20

The Protestant denominations of the United States and Canada have determined upon certain major objectives or purposes in the religious nurture of life; these may be phrased differently from time to time, and particular aspects may be lifted up as applying especially at certain age levels, but the general areas present inescapable challenge:

Knowledge of God which is true to Christian teaching and a growing consciousness of fellowship with this Christlike God.

Knowledge and understanding of Jesus which will lead to personal commitment to Him.

A philosophy of life which is warmly and positively Christian. Growth in Christlike habits.

Ability to live as a Christian in society, beginning first of all in one's home.

Ability to participate actively in the church fellowship.

Knowledge of the Bible which is dynamic and which leads to zest for continuous Bible study.

The important idea in these goals is that persons be led into growing fellowship with God as Father, and with others as brothers —not merely in intellectual assent but in *practice*. As to the way such fellowship is achieved, there may be many paths. For some there may be climactic experiences, for others gradual dawnings without marked crises through Christian nurture in home and church. The two streams of Christian education and evangelism come together in the concept of guiding persons toward God, after the example of Jesus.

A worker may visualize these goals by placing a young person in the center in his imagination; surrounding him are ever-expanding circles of human relationships: first his family, next his close friends, his play groups and clubs, then school, church, community, world. Cutting through all these relationships, like spokes of a wheel, are the areas or goals suggested above. If attempt is made to leave one relationship out, the goal is not realized. Christianity must apply to all of life. It cannot be compartmentalized. This picture with

21

spokes cutting through all the circles of one's daily life appears like a pilot's wheel, symbolizing each individual's learning to pilot his own life. The church's job is to help him learn from the Master Pilot to steer with poise and sureness toward Christlike goals for himself and society.

No clearer, sterner, nor more provocative statement of goals for Christian education of youth was ever given than Jesus' reply to the question, "Teacher, which is the great commandment in the law?"

And he said to him, "You shall love the Lord your God with all your heart, and with all your soul, and with all your mind. This is the great and first commandment. And a second is like it, You shall love your neighbor as yourself. On these two commandments depend all the law and the prophets."[1]

In this statement are the three focal points: God—then others, and self, as seen in new light because of relationship to God.

But not all that goes under the name of the church program may contribute to the realization of these aims. Only as parents and all others who teach and counsel youth in home and church take seriously their responsibilities, use the best possible methods, and seek ever to evaluate what they do by the Master Teacher will the affirmed goals become realities; will the Word become flesh and dwell among us. Home and church working together are challenged to: (1) command the respect of young people; (2) channel their energies; (3) cultivate their intelligence; and (4) call them to high commitment to the Christian way. —But *how?* Below are some implications for local church work with young people; workers and parents meeting often together and considering carefully and prayerfully their aims will think of other implications.

That Young People May Be Helped to Put God First in Their Lives

Until they center their lives in the Living God, young people need not expect to be able to "make sense" out of the scattered pieces of their lives and the gigantic puzzle of their world.

The church's program for youth should not be merely "youth-centered." Youth themselves should be helped to center in One

22

higher. To be sure, any good leader of youth will discover and use their current interests as a *starting point* in methods; but he will not stop or center there. Sometimes his function as adult friend is to prod, awaken, and stimulate to greater and higher interests; and to an awareness of deeper needs. Young people have two gravitational relationships: the vertical, to God; the horizontal, to others. They need the kind of program activities that stir them to grow in these dimensions.

Something happens in an individual life when he decides to put God first. Selfish interests fall off like dead leaves in the spring. Desires that formerly pulled in conflicting directions now pull together. Personality becomes forceful. Neuropsychiatric wards of hospitals abound in young patients who are there, the doctors say, because they lack a "dominant center" for organizing their powers.

Something happens in a group of young people when they decide they will try to put God first. The group begins to glow as if with inner fire. Like a magnet, it attracts others. Attendance increases, not from artificial means such as drives, but because those who come feel they are touching reality. They *get* something, something they have been hungry for all along but did not know it. "Souls restless . . . until they find their rest in Thee."[2]

That church that decides to put first in its planning this need of young people for a centering in God, may find it necessary to make some changes of focus in its program, that it may:

1. *Affirm before the community at large its unique function as the church of the Living God.* If the church bids for the respect of young people, let it not be apologetic. Let its architecture proclaim fearlessly the upreach of the soul toward God. (Many church buildings, had they no bulletin boards, might be taken for libraries or courthouses or schools, maybe even jails.) Church methods need not imitate those of theater or gambling joint in order to get attendance. When other agencies of the community demand much of youth's time, should the church meekly cut down on its schedule and demand less of their time? Should church workers with youth appear satisfied with poor workmanship as youth take part in church activi-

ties? Rather, church meetings should be made so vital and their importance so affirmed that young people will come to choose them of their own accord. Let the church speak forth its central message with tremendous power. Let it proclaim that it does have the answer to youth's deepest needs.

2. *Devote more care and attention to training young people in the worship of God.* Some church programs with youth—imitating those of schools, clubs, and other agencies—become so crammed full of activities that worship is all but crowded out. A young president announced to his fellow officers at council meeting, "We have so many items to discuss at this meeting that we will just dispense with the opening worship." Hundreds of churches have put thousands, maybe millions, of dollars into expensive recreational and social equipment but have left their intermediates, their seniors, and their older youth no meeting places of their own conducive to worship and the worship training they need on their own age levels.

Little wonder then that young people seem not to know how to pray. Little wonder that they appear to feel no inner urgency, many of them, to participate in church services of worship. Everyone in his growing years needs to be guided in learning *how* to worship, with emphasis always upon the central experience of fellowship with God rather than upon the periphery of programizing. Many youth are adept at "getting up and leading," but lost when it comes to the simplest acts of worship.

The pastor has some opportunity with his preparatory church membership class. But he himself has probably not been trained in methods of teaching and guiding younger persons; he probably is not aware of the units along these same lines in the regular ongoing curriculum. He probably has but little time to spend. Often he will likely succumb to the temptation to use words that are unclear to young minds and to fall back on old lecture and even catechetical methods at the expense of deeper, richer learning experiences the youth might have with better methods. Such classes, helpful as they are, cannot do the whole job in guiding youth in ways of worshiping God.

Every church should make a careful plan for worship guidance up through the years, as the very *heart* of that church's work. Few churches have faced up to this opportunity as yet. Too often, the worship guidance is a hit-or-miss matter; with older departments, the counselors "get up a program" or expect the young people to do so, following probably some canned worked-out services from books or other printed materials. Vital worship guidance is an entirely different matter; it starts with the meaning of worship and prayer; it opens to young hearts the naturalness of fellowship with God and His accessibility at all times; it suggests ways all members of a group may help each other by being in a spirit of prayer; it minimizes formal programs or "leading"; it urges sincerity of expression rather than reading or memorizing "parts" from outside sources.

For each age-group department above the children's division there should be "worship counselors" trained carefully over a long period of time by the pastor. He should consider such training his mainline opportunity as "spiritual shepherd" of the entire church flock.

Opportunities should be incorporated into the total church schedule for varied types of worship guidance: in the classes or discussion groups, as young people are led to pause naturally for prayer; in their informal meetings of their own age level Sunday morning, evening, or other times; and in the larger corporate service of the whole church family with its awesome note and its use of worship customs and materials from the church of the ages.[3]

3. *Demand that workers with youth be persons of high spiritual qualifications.* An old book of biography tells about "men of the burning heart" whose lives in turn enkindled fires of Christian purpose in the young lives they touched. Young people often meet in their daily walks of life grownups who are cynical, who lack moral fiber. Only to their church can they look for assurance that ideals *can* be translated into life. Religion is more caught than taught. So is irreligion.

Young people need to be associated with persons who themselves are in awe before the great truths of life; before the epic grandeur of the story of God in the Bible and in church history; before goodness in people no matter how humble. Young people need leaders who themselves practice daily devotions—not that they would talk

25

much about it, but the habit will show through their more poised, winsome personalities, and through the attitudes they take on crucial issues. Young people will know if they have merely read some suggestions out of a book from which they are teaching, or if they have spent some time with God and have absorbed into themselves something of the "mind that was in Christ Jesus."

4. *Revive hymn singing!* Why should not young people be taught to sing with fervor the great hymns of the church? Great movements in church history have been marked by creative hymnic expression and fervent singing by the masses. The great hymns of the faith can unite youth in fellowship with one another, and with the Christians of all the ages, and call forth their aspirations to the high and holy today.[4]

5. *Provide unhurried time.* Young people need a chance to "be still and know." They need to get away from noise and rush that fill their days. Some are seeking this chance in spiritual life retreats—retreats *from* the unreality and artificiality of thing-centered days *to* the fresh, healing, and life-giving reality of a sojourn in deeper fellowship with one another and with God. Some church schedules of youth activities could be streamlined and simplified, to give a straighter drive toward a few central goals that are the church's special business and cutting out any overlapping of what school and clubs are doing. "Termites" that eat up precious time in church meetings can be exterminated: starting late, lack of preparation, unnecessary announcements, etc.

6. *Call young persons to "spiritual athleticism."* Some young persons today are undertaking exacting disciplines of prayer and action reminiscent of the saints of old, that they might develop spiritual stamina and strength for tests more grueling than the Olympics as they seek to bring about Christian practices in a stubborn world. They gather in spiritual life retreats, form "fellowships of concern" or prayer cells. They generate a power that makes itself felt on countless campuses and in communities throughout the world. They keep in touch with similar groups across oceans. Already youth have an unofficial interdenominational and international prayer fellowship. They do not stop with evangelistic effort in their own home

26

towns, but board cattle boats or go on missions of teaching or enter work camps. They study the causes of strikes, hunger, unemployment, erosion, prejudice, disease, wars. Their energies are straining to get at the world's maladies with healing measures.

Can the church call more of them? Can it lead them in their disciplines, that they not make of disciplines ends in themselves and not veer off onto tangential interests? When young persons gather and ask probing questions; when they focus incisive minds on roots of problems—will adult workers be found who themselves are sufficiently tough-minded and fearless and informed and disciplined to *go with the young people* on such quests? When the courage of young folks lags, will there be adult friends to whom they can look who themselves are climbing ever higher in spiritual adventuring?

That the Church May Foster Good Clear Thinking and Wise Christian Action

Young persons need to learn better *how* to think! —*How* to ferret out problems and define them clearly, how to search for and use aids, how to bring to bear the searchlight of the Christian faith, how to discuss, how to decide, how to act. Little use telling young people the answer to today's problems. Tomorrow's will be different! What they need is a *way* of facing all problems. How may the church seek to do a better job along this line?

1. *Provide time and guidance in problem-solving in the classes and meetings of youth.* Units of study and discussion for Sunday school and evening meeting, as they appear in the recommended curriculum, suggest problem solving. The adult worker can help build an atmosphere of free, frank friendliness in which each young person can express his mind without fear or hesitation. There should be sufficient blocks of time (forty-five minutes as the extreme minimum in the Sunday school; longer in the evening meeting) so that young people can dig below the surface of a problem. The adult guides, never forces. He does not *tell* the young people what with a little help they could find out for themselves. He does not *do* for them what with a little help they could do for themselves.

Together in these intimate small fellowships, adult friend and young minds *come to grips* with the meaning of Christianity today. To keep discussion on a "strictly neutral" plane is deadening. To fear to face controversial issues is paralyzing. Jesus took stands. To deal in vague abstractions or pious-sounding generalities is to anaesthetize. Too many young people have learned through school and other agencies to "look at all sides of a question"—but never to come to grips, make up their minds, and take their stand! Christian living today demands decisiveness. Teaching should be "for a verdict!"

Good thinking is not fostered by mere discussion without the needed facts or resources. Young people need to be trained in how to find and use resources. They should not be allowed to form habits of premature judgments (prejudice) without proper information. The teachings of the Christian religion should be brought into their thinking positively and not apologetically. The world needs persons who can *think* as Christians.

2. *Provide a sustaining fellowship.* Young people who seek to follow the Christian way will be lonely. They may be unpopular in their groups. They need the sustaining fellowship of others of like decision. This need is for something deeper than organization: a kinship deepened by shared worship, by searching discussion, and by concerns felt and answered together. Members "bear each other up." Alcoholics Anonymous and other groups make use of the psychology of mutual responsibility. John Wesley's "class meetings" afforded to the new converts a sustaining fellowship; the members encouraged one another to persevere. Has the church of today, in its zeal for numbers and in its administrative and organizational efficiency, sometimes failed to foster this deeper fellowship of the spirit?

Sadly, sometimes "spiritual things are done in unspiritual ways."[5] Tensions arise between members of a church group, or between groups. Officers get cumbered about many things and tend to forget the "one thing most needful." Youth become efficient in "running" activities but lack this deeper fellowship, this *koinonia*.

3. *Guide young people in following through into action.* Too much of the time, young people meet at the church on Sundays and

talk or worship *about* problems, but fail to follow through in positive action. Too many large conventions of youth in the past have been resolutionary rather than revolutionary. Whenever a group, local or larger, contents itself with talking and fails to move out into arenas of human relationships, that group may be substituting a dream world for the real; words for work. Gaining a purple glow of security from deciding what *should* be done is an unhealthy spiritual state; there should be desperate insecurity until positive action results.

Space prohibits listing areas of community and world life where inspired young people *have* made a difference. Clear-eyed youth can sometimes see causes for evils when adults might tend to rationalize the evils away. Courageous youth will dare try when adults might say, "Nothing can be done."

Some junior high school clubs[6] run on the principle that no topic will be brought into meeting for discussion that the members are unwilling to follow through in action. This club has effected a playground in a slum area of a city, averted gang warfare, and done other amazing "real jobs in a real world." Church meetings and classes might be revolutionized if members came, not just to "have a lesson," or "put on a program," but in order to gather information for needed action. Then from action they would come back for further light and for strength that comes from worship and fellowship. Faith—works; roots—fruits; diastole—systole of the heartbeat of real religion.

Before young people will move out thus, their parents and other adult helpers must be willing to move with them. Young people need workers who will let them dream dreams *above* the level of the present horizon. Christian guidance fails if it produces only a generation of adapters to the status quo. It should generate "creative Christian non-conformists."[7]

That Idealism May Be Nurtured in Young Minds and Hearts

In a crassly technological age, young persons need to have their deeper feelings fostered, and not alone their mental outreach. The

29

"dream power" of youth is precious. It needs much nourishment, as does a tender plant in blinding light.

Young sensitivities should be exposed to that which is moving, and high and holy: the great in music, in art, in drama, in life. Young people should be led to experience emotional identification with others whose folk songs and games they enjoy, and to whom their missionary offerings go.

Consciences should grow sharp as young people are guided to evaluate their lives and present conditions in relation to that Most Perfect Life. Only thus can they become the Christian conscience for society. Rather than being protected from the cruel facts of others' sufferings and needs, young people should *know* and *feel,* even until it hurts and hurts deeply. Then they may want so much to help that they will *find* a way to rid the world of causes of sufferings in wars and hatreds.

The epic grandeur of the Old Testament, the red-blooded hero stories of Paul and early Christians, the moving drama of the church through the ages—all these should be in youth's religious menu.

Merely attempting to inculcate traits is not the way. A trait or characteristic may be learned after a fashion by concentration upon itself as an end. But the inner motive at the heart is the important thing. One grows more helpful or virtuous by simply loving others until one *wants* to help; or by holding the Christian ideal until one naturally decides for high levels of living. "Adaptability" may sound like a desirable characteristic. But there are times when a Christian should *not* be weakly adaptable. "Loyalty" may sound like a worthy ideal. But loyalty harnessed to wrong causes or persons is dangerous.

Great Christians have always "marched to the beat of a different drummer"—not merely to be different or to set themselves apart from the crowd. There is a difference for a young person between isolating himself to get attention, and standing firmly yet humbly for a Christian cause as he sees it whether anyone stands with him or not. The prophets were nonconformists with the prevalent way of living of their day. The business of the church is not to furnish cushions

30

of security, but rather to keep tensions alive—in such areas as war, race, industry, where Christian thought and action are needed.

The entire youth program of the church should culminate in vocational choices made (1) in the light of the world's needs, (2) according to personal abilities, and (3) in sincere effort to find and make full commitment to the will of God. The range of choices is vast. From 338 vocations in 1870 there were listed 20,000 possibilities in the Occupational Dictionary of the United States Department of Labor in 1940. Young people can study vocational fields in the light of the Christian ideal, asking themselves in which walks one can "live as a full-time Christian." Full-time church vocations include administrators, missionaries, ministers, directors of religious education and the like over the world. In worthy walks of life, young Christians can seek to transform "from the inside" the dealings of man with man—as farmers, businessmen, politicians, homemakers, nurses, doctors, teachers, journalists, governmental leaders, diplomats, ambassadors, economists, etc.

Let youth work in the churches, then, have a cutting edge! Let special cultivation be given those potential leaders capable of rising above the level of usual activities. Jesus developed a few for special tasks. Too much of church work with youth in the past has moved on ordinary or average levels. Special guidance should be given ones fitted by temperament, interests, and commitment to be the spiritual pioneers, the frontiersmen, the mystics, the artists, the hymn writers, the great thinkers, the direction setters of the church and world of tomorrow.

I am a Dream in the Soul of Youth.
In the soul of youth everywhere I have always found myself at home.
I make eyes turn away from the little things of today to the greater things of tomorrow.
I give wistfulness to the face, grip to the hands, unconscious beauty to the form, and iron to the ribbing of the soul.
I make youth so forgetful of itself that it becomes inevitably beautiful.
As I have slowly conquered the soul of youth, I have thereby changed the world.
And someday . . .

Listen to me, ye men and women who glut your greed on the rights of others, ye forces of hate that control mankind, ye iron souls of Force that gloat in your power and success, ye ghoulish fiends of Poverty, and Ignorance, and Prejudice—

Someday, I will completely capture the soul of youth—and then I will say unto you—the Temple of man's soul was meant to be a house of Beauty and of Prayer, but ye have made it a Den of Thievery and of Hell. In the name of Christ get ye out, and get ye out now.

And ye will get out, because, mark you, no force like mine has ever before challenged your right to work your will upon mankind.

I am a Dream in the Soul of Youth.[8]

III

LONG-RANGE PLANNING
IN THE CHURCH

Sanctify them through thy truth: thy word is truth.
JOHN 17:17

What is the church's "program" for young people? The "program" is wherever a young person is: yonder there in the back alley where a girl named "Tomboy" plots with her gang for hair-raising escapades. The "program" is also in a quiet home where a girl is practicing her music so as to be able someday to play the organ in church. The "program" is in the school where, against the tide of accepted patterns regarding cheating, one young person stands firmly for an ideal. The "program" is in a social party where a young person refuses to touch a proffered flask. The "program" is in a group conversation where disparaging things are being said about representatives of another nationality, and a young person of the church speaks a good word kindly.

And beyond the present reach of the "church program" are thousands upon thousands of unreached, floundering without guidance as to how to live, how to pray, how to decide. Somehow those in whom the "program" now lives must extend the reach to others.

Actually, the minutes provided in the usual Sunday school, evening meeting, or other youth gathering in the church are merely a "checking of signals"—for the important part is the going out to live as Christ-centered young persons. What are some important ways the local church seeks to help its young people thus live? The following represent a cross section in terms of *experiences* young persons may have in the church. All of these are available to the little class of six in a one-room church, if they add to their times of learning and worship Sunday mornings, some projects of service action, occasional recreation, and the like. In larger churches with more periods when youth meet, it will be obviously easier to provide for these full-rounded experiences.

1. *Opportunity to worship God, and guidance that they may grow in their understanding of what it means to worship and pray.* Young people need God. The way to find Him and to grow in fellowship with Him is through worship and prayer. They learn to worship and pray through guided practice.

In churches large enough to provide separate meeting space on Sunday mornings for their younger and older youth, this guidance can be by age levels. In one-room churches, Sunday school teachers can help instruct in ways of worshiping. Occasional extra meetings in homes may provide more time. Worshiping with the church congregation should be considered a normal part of the growing worship life of young people. They need, in addition, simpler, more informal worship experiences with others of similar age and needs. They need guidance for individual devotions.

2. *Opportunity to study, investigate, discuss, learn, interpret, decide.* This can be true of the smallest church as of the largest. The two major periods for learning are the class time on Sunday mornings and the evening session.

Young people of each age level need separate meeting rooms and classes. When grouped with others of differing ages and interests, their expression is not as free. No one knows how many young people have dropped out because of loneliness in uncongenial church groupings.

This book deals primarily with guidance of young people in learning experiences, taking into account that prayer is a natural part of the search for truth; and that learning, worship, recreation, and service cannot be separated in the texture of Christian growth.

3. *Opportunity for guided recreation.* This can be true of the smallest church as of the largest. Intermediates need one kind of recreational guidance (games, hobbies, etc., that call for more physical activity); seniors another kind (skilled games); older youth another kind (folk games, mental contests, more sophisticated fun). Intermediates and seniors need more help from their adult counselors in planning for and directing their recreation. In addition, young

34

people of all ages need guidance in setting up criteria for selection of recreational pursuits in their individual lives and in their groups outside the church.

4. *Opportunity to form worthy habits of serving and giving.* This can be true of the smallest church as of the largest. Intermediates can be guided to do things for their parents, their church, for any others close around them—simple, everyday service acts. Seniors and older youth can undertake longer-term, and more far-reaching service projects. All youth should be helped to form habits of giving systematically to the work of their local churches and to the world-wide mission of the church. There should be developing within them a sincere friendly attitude toward others near and far, and a motive of helpfulness and goodwill, stretching from community to world, and across all barriers.

5. *Opportunity to deepen Christian fellowship.* Intermediates, seniors, and older youth can learn to carry responsibilities—caring more about doing the job well than about winning credit for themselves. Harmony should exist between the young people and their adult workers, and among the members of the group. There should be a warm friendliness, a genuine *esprit d'corps,* a plus element of good fellowship. Especially should their group life extend to others as yet unreached, in genuine eagerness to share the good things of the Christian way with them. Christian brotherhood, to become a reality in larger world relationships, must first be practiced in smaller group relationships. The church-school classes, committees, and other gatherings of young people offer splendid "laboratories" for such practice!

How translate these opportunities into a schedule of church activities? Granted that home teaching is first—that in their homes young people are being guided steadily, continuously, and powerfully—for better or for worse. And granted that community influences surround every young life with a welter of forces pulling this way and that. What, specifically, can the church do and when and how? How blueprint goals into schedules and plans? Let us look at some possibilities in the not-too-extraordinary church situation.

9:45–11:00 SUNDAY CHURCH SCHOOL
Worship—approximately 15 minutes.

Possible learnings: deepened beliefs about the nature of God; helps in use of resources such as hymns in worship; habits of reverence or irreverence; desire for fuller fellowship with Him and willingness to seek His will; growing understanding of prayer and worship as communion with God.

Classes—approximately 50-60 minutes (in some churches, because of wasting of time earlier, the inclusion of long instructional talks or stories in the devotional period, and general poor planning, classes may have only 20 minutes or so—what incentive to teachers or youth?).

Possible learnings: how to discuss together problems of Christian living; how to use the Bible and other resources; how to think and decide; how to plan and carry through enterprises; how to have richer fellowship with one another in the group and with other groups.

11:00–12:00 WORSHIP WITH THE CHURCH CONGRE-GATION
Possible experiences: larger group fellowship; giving; learnings (from the sermon, the symbols, the hymns, the ritual, the sacraments, the Scripture); worship.

6:00– 7:30 EVENING MEETING
Possible learnings: how to transact business and make plans; how to discuss intelligently and arrive at conclusions on problems of personal and social Christian living; how to worship; how to pray in groups; how to carry ideas into action; how to interpret the mind of Christ in today's life. Possible experiences: group fellowship; serving and giving; recreation (in some churches it is preferred to have all recreation on a

36

weekday; whenever provided, it should be considered a vital and meaningful part of a well-rounded "program" and not merely a way of attracting or holding youth).

Other potential learnings will suggest themselves as interested parents and teachers observe what their churches are doing, or failing to do, in the total offering of activities in an average week.

Other potential learnings are there, not shown in the above picture and not so desirable. By failing to start on time, a youth group may be *learning* to come late and to regard church activities as relatively insignificant. By contenting themselves with poorly-prepared worship services, young people may be learning not to take their opportunities for worship seriously or to *expect* to meet with the Most High God when they gather together. By dealing casually through poorly-prepared reading "parts" in their meetings with the great moving truths of the Christian religion for which martyrs have given their lives, young people may be learning a blasé, so-what attitude toward the greatest things of life. By skimming lightly over great and crucial problems, they may be learning *not* to think rigorously about applying religion to life. By becoming satisfied with having had a program on a social issue, they may be learning *not* to continue to be concerned until wise and well-planned action matches the problem.

Therefore, it behooves all church workers with young people and parents to meet often together and look carefully and prayerfully—not just at the *surface* of their church's work, but in so far as possible at the inner learnings that are taking place. Church work can do *harm* to young lives!

Youth Workers in a Church Meet and Plan Together

In a very small church, there may be just one teacher of the younger youth, and possibly one for the older ones. They with their minister should plan together, and invite one or more parents to meet with them, to bring in the point of view of the home.

In larger churches, workers with young people may be more numerous and may serve in more varied capacities. Whatever their title, they are all "teachers" in the deepest sense. These may include: youth division superintendents, counselors for age-group departments, teachers in the Sunday morning sessions, leaders in expanded or additional sessions, counselors for evening meetings, advisers to committees or commissions, pianists, record-keepers, club leaders (Scouts, Camp Fire Girls, etc.), representative parents, pastor, general church-school superintendent.

All workers with young people in *any* church should meet often together to "see the program whole," as it is affecting the lives of the young persons to whom they are attempting to minister. Does this imply that *adults* are urged to meet and plan? Would that not rob youth of "participation"? No! Clear thinking will suggest that this over-all survey and general planning by adult workers in no wise overlaps youth's own areas for planning. There are some things youth cannot do! Likewise, there are some things—those within the experience range and abilities of the age level of youth involved—adults should not rob them of their chance to do. But short-sighted "letting youth do it all" may mean failure on the part of adult workers to attain a level of youth work worthy of a Christian church!

Of concern for all "teachers" of youth in any church are these imperatives:

1. To study the needs, problems, and interests of the young people of their church; to read or hear book reviews and learn of other helpful materials to guide them in their relationships with their youth; to hear from experts who have studied youth of the different ages; to confer with parents, club leaders, and schoolteachers working with these same young folk.

2. To study what should be the general goals of all church work with young people, and with each age level; to receive guidance from qualified leaders about theology, and renew their own awareness of the basic beliefs of the Christian faith; to consider these beliefs in relation to the curriculum used, their methods and their Christian example.

3. To consider principles and policies for youth work in their church that should be talked over with the young people for their

38

viewpoints, and recommended to the church official body responsible for the total program of Christian education.

4. To study what their church is now doing with each age level with a view to making the best possible use of time schedule, room space, and equipment, printed materials, and organization.

5. To study the curriculum materials provided by their denomination for the Sunday school, evening meetings, weekday sessions, vacation school, camp, story papers, and the like. To make recommendations to the youth officers and to the church board of education so that orders for proper materials for each age level may be sent in sufficiently early for workers and young people to have sufficient time to prepare their units well in advance.

6. To study the available room space and equipment, to determine ways for making the most effective use possible of what is available and for suggesting recommendations for improvement.

7. To plan for the next forthcoming units of study and worship *together*—that is, workers in the Sunday school and workers in the evening meeting going over materials for both sessions and helping each other plan, so that for the young people themselves their work may be a "living whole" instead of two wholly unrelated parts sometimes overlapping and sometimes leaving out important areas.

8. To evaluate methods used in teaching and counseling, with a view to conserving the values of earlier training the young people have had through the children's division; and with a view to preparing them for experiences they will face as adults.

9. To plan for ways of celebrating great days and seasons of the church year, so as to open for the young people doorways into highly meaningful experiences.

10. To give consideration to any personal or special needs arising among individuals; and to seek to meet problem situations in such a way as to make them steppingstones forward.

11. To co-operate with the pastor in preparing young people for church membership, and in helping them find places for active service in the church.

12. To study community and other influences impinging upon

young lives; to seek counsel with leaders of youth in other agencies and to work out means for co-operation in eradicating community evils and promoting character growth in the youth of the community.

13. To co-operate with other age-group departments of the church school and with all-church enterprises. To seek to help youth extend their interests and loyalties to the work of the whole church, and not alone of their youth fellowship.

14. To encourage one another as workers with youth to take advantage of all possible opportunities for growth: leadership courses in schools and through correspondence; informal meetings and conferences with persons who can help; recommended reading; films; etc.

15. To keep in touch with connectional workers of the denomination who may give helpful advice through correspondence or visits.

16. To hear reports of committees, commissions, interest groups, or individuals who have taken special responsibilities.

17. To give attention to the financial program with youth, and to consider whether Christian beliefs and habits of stewardship of money are being fostered.

18. To clear dates on the all-church calendar.

19. Etc.

Each Worker Is Related to the Total Youth Program

Thus, the entire church program for and with its young people "teaches." All who help in any way are "teachers." Probably no real teacher of young people has ever counted his work done when he has taught, or met with a group for a certain number of minutes on a Sunday, closed his quarterly, and gone home. He carries concern for each young person in his heart all the time. Not only when he is meeting with them, but all the time, he is "their teacher."

When pastor and superintendent recruit workers, they should make it clear that any job with young people involves a relationship to the total youth program. No one is to plow a lone furrow. Each teacher, counselor, adviser, or helper becomes a member of a working *staff*. Ideal, yes. But hard common sense, too. For unless one participates in the total planning, and sees youth work whole, he is likely not to do well his own specific part.

40

This does not mean that the same person is necessarily asked to assume responsibility both for a Sunday school class or department and for the Sunday evening meeting. Division of labor is wise, although when persons *do* have sufficient time and commitment to take both jobs, there is more unity. But so important is *any* post of service with young people that probably *one* meeting is all a worker can do and do exceeding well. Better that several different persons be recruited, with no one overloaded, and with all planning in utmost co-operation, so that the program is one body that lives and breathes!

Problems of Room Space and Equipment

Here is an intermediate class meeting Sunday after Sunday in a crowded choir loft, with chairs on different tiers. Here is a small senior class meeting in a church kitchen, hampered by smelly damp dishrags and overhanging pots. Here are five classes meeting in a large gymnasium, with hubbub dinning on ears and nerves of youth and workers alike.

Lack of certain minimum essentials of room and equipment handicaps the learning process more than can be measured. It says to the young people with undeniable eloquence, "Your church considers you of minor importance." Perhaps these young people will in turn consider the church of minor importance in their scheme of things. When building or remodeling, church committees should seek the insights and practical suggestions of *church consultants*. Local architects used to building for secular enterprises generally are not aware of important considerations for *church* work. Millions of dollars are spent yearly with an alarming high percentage of inadequate equipment resulting, that will handicap the church experiences of young people for generations to come![1] A *minimum* essential for any church is provision for separate age-level rooms.

Stories multiply, to be sure, of ways youth groups manage to carry on after a fashion under needlessly adverse conditions: in a back corner of a one-room church with two pews and a wall space; in a blocked-off corner of a side vestibule; in bell tower; in furnace room. What is accomplished in spite of handicaps is but pitiful evidence as to what *might* be done with better equipment. Unbelievable is the short-sightedness of ministers and committees who set up gymnasia, show movies, or resort to other desperate measures to "attract" young people while failing to provide for them attractive meeting rooms for their mainline Sunday meetings in the church! The best possible way for youth workers to convince church boards as to needs is to make such exhaustive use of present equipment as to overflow its bounds in attendance and activities. Lack of space or equipment is never an excuse for failure to use better methods. But often, inappropriate and frustrating surroundings do destroy morale, lessen youth's interest in church activities, and cut down on their joy.

A new teacher came into a senior department in which morale was low. The theme was, "We can't . . ." One Sunday morning this worker brought a picture for the worship period. She had searched carefully to find beauty without expense. The picture spoke a message that morning. Young people gathered afterward and asked, "May we keep it here?"

But immediately, they saw that the walls were too dirty for that picture. "Let's clean up!" was the decision. A cabinet was made for supplies by one of the boys. The piano was relieved of its dusty burden of hymnals, story papers, and Bibles. A wall drape of inexpensive cloth was made by the girls and hung as background for pictures and to lend depth to the appearance of the room. Courage gained, both the young people and their workers "perked up." "We can," they had decided.

Problems as to Time Schedule

Schedules are made for young people, not young people for schedules. If the present allotted time for Sunday school class or evening meeting proves inadequate, let the young people themselves decide what to do about it. Usually, where interest is at a sufficiently high level, their request for more time will be spontaneous.

It is not wise to attempt to organize an evening meeting until the age group has first become so interested in activities begun on Sunday morning that they *want* to come back for additional time. They will then have a *reason* for the extra meeting. Workers who say, "Attendance and interest at Sunday school is low. We must therefore set up an evening meeting," are foolish. Let them first study the *causes* for the failure; build up the present work until enthusiasm spills over; find and train more workers to do a better job *before* setting up meetings that will require more and better leadership.

A group of older young people may decide to use their Sunday evening meeting to continue discussion begun at Sunday school. Intermediates may need some time Sunday afternoon or evening to complete their activities. Why a "traditional" *program* in evening meetings merely as routine? To be sure, in setting up their yearly calendar, the age group may have allocated for evening meetings certain units important in their cycle. All plans within the total schedule should be "loose" enough to be adapted to the needs of a group at a given time. "We're just dying to talk with somebody about that problem," remarked Jane, "but we can't, because we have to have our meeting now." Why should young people feel enslaved by a time schedule, or by the phobia that because certain kinds of meetings have always been held at a certain hour, they will always have to be?

The main problem is blindness as to good methods for *both* Sunday morning and Sunday evening when the old teacher-lecture method is used in the mornings and the old youth-read-part method is used in the evenings with net result of poor learnings at either time. It should be understood that activities of learning belong as fully and richly in the morning session as in the evening. The only difference is that in some churches, space is more crowded in the mornings and each group must take into account the presence of the others. But in basic essentials for the learning process, schedule should not dictate method.

Young people are busy, yes. Sometimes it seems hard to get them to come for Sunday mornings and Sunday evenings. Sometimes they come tense and hurried, overstimulated. While every minute of their time at church should be full of reality, workers themselves should never appear rushed, and should never allow the young people to feel so. Each meeting should have about it something of the fresh clean breath of open spaces and the unhurriedness of God's eternal plans. Growth cannot be forced into a time schedule. In quietness and confidence shall be a young person's strength.

IV

FELLOWSHIP: YOUTH WITH
THEIR WORKERS

*From whom the whole body fitly joined together and compacted
by that which every joint supplieth, according to the effectual
working in the measure of every part, maketh increase of the body
unto the edifying of itself in love.* EPHESIANS 4:16

A teacher does not teach a class or group. He works with *individuals,* who may gather at times in classes or groups. In each life, God is already there long before the teacher comes upon the scene. Each individual is unique in God's sight. He should be so in the teacher's sight. But in the togetherness persons experience when they gather in groups can be seen the hand of God at work also. The teacher's task is to seek ever to understand and co-operate with the workings of God, both in individual lives and in group fellowship.

Seeking to Understand How Young Persons Grow

To study adolescence means to study *adolescents.* Let the reader hold in his mind a mental picture of some of the young individuals in whose spiritual growth he is most interested. What motives propel them in their restless round of activity? Along what lines are their interests running this current month? What forms of recreation do they prefer? What ideas are they forming from their school studies? What set of values is community life holding up before them? What is their attitude toward parents, teachers, and adults in general? How have their homes influenced them to date? What are some of their innermost ambitions?

Any great adventure in human relationships takes time. One cannot go out in a brief half hour and get acquainted with his intermediates, his seniors, or his older youth. The more time he devotes, the greater will be his rewards. A photographer sometimes devotes many patient hours to getting the perfect shot. Let not a teacher begrudge time from his own weekly schedule for visiting in the homes of his young people, for dropping casually into the drugstore when the bunch is out of school, for being there cheering when the big game comes off. Soon he will discover that what matters greatly to his young people will matter to him, too!

Notes will help the worker remember what might otherwise slip away. Each person has his own comfortable way of note-taking. A loose-leaf or card arrangement is easily handled and permits additions. Notes kept from year to year, tracing the growth of individuals, may be passed on to the next teacher. The work of the church can thus be put on a more businesslike and scientific basis. In his notebook, the teacher may place first some general pages for basic characteristics of his age level; ideas he has found that deepen his understanding of them (from his reading, his use of church periodicals, leadership courses, and the like). On separate pages, he will write the name, address, and birthday of each young person with whom he works. These pages will grow as information is gained. On James Jones' page will go records of visits in the home; of birthdays (young people like to receive greetings and reassurance that their teacher cares about them personally); of questions Jim brought up in the group, or in personal conversation; of responsibilities he has taken or refused; of his general attitudes in the group and of others' attitudes toward him; of indications he has given of "growing edges."

Such a notebook is secret and kept utterly confidential. The teacher will guard its contents, and guard himself from speaking thoughtlessly to others about Jim. When Jim is to be promoted, the teacher will pass on to the next one his notebook; he in turn will add. One teacher keeps his notes with his Bible and other personal devotional materials. Opening the notebook to the page about Jim, he holds Jim up in prayer in the Presence of One who cares for all, and seeks fresh insights as to how to be the kind of adult friend Jim needs.

To grow in his understanding of young persons as individuals, the teacher will seek to view them from as many angles as possible:

1. *Viewing them first, to the extent possible, through their own eyes.* No adult can do that, fully. He is too cumbered with his own

46

accumulated experiences. But he can note: questions that have come forth spontaneously; motives this young person may unconsciously reveal, even while "covering up"; dominant interests to which he gives most time; groups he enjoys being with. An adult must needs often read "between the lines" of what a young person says or does.

Teachers in training classes are sometimes asked to list "needs of youth." At first, they tend to list needs they think the young people *ought* to feel—as viewed from their own vantage point as adults. When they go out to interview young people and come back with needs youth themselves express the list may be quite different!

The products of young minds and hands also help reveal their real selves: things they write; collections they make; awards they achieve in clubs to which they belong; activities in which they participate from choice, such as drama or music. One teacher calls himself a collector of "youth-alia" (writings and drawings of youth).

The adult friend of youth will find it a stern and difficult discipline, but an ever-rewarding one, to try to view a young person in terms of his own estimate of himself—not the group's estimate or the teacher's own first estimate. There is no such thing as a "problem young person." There is a young person with a problem. Danny disrupts the class. The first reaction is to label Danny, "disrupter of my plans!" But let her get her own reactions out of the way. Danny is a miserable young person suffering from lack of home affectional security. Only as the teacher can see Danny as he is, will she be in a position to offer understanding and help. Parents sometimes need to look beyond the smoke screen of their own reactions ("Stop annoying me now!") to the problem that may be annoying their offspring. Before considering a young person "unco-operative," let the teacher pause to ask if after all it is so important that his (the teacher's) plans be co-operated with, as that this youngster be helped on concerns important to *him*.

Adolescents live in a world of their own. Sometimes they manage rather cleverly to barricade this world against adult intrusion. Secret dreams and griefs are camouflaged. Unless the adult be alert, he

47

may mistake the camouflage for the real thing. He may treat symptoms rather than causes.

This wave length of their own that adolescents maintain is a part of their protective mechanism against the outside world. Gangs of adolescents have a "cult" of their own—the strange-sounding words they use with one another, the interminable phone calls; the front porch giggling and whispered conversations that issue in picnics, parties, dates.

Yet there is a wistfulness to be accepted by the grown-up world. "My parents ought to understand me better," asserts fifteen-year-old Bob energetically. He and his sister Jane rush to get the monthly copy of *Parents' Magazine* before their parents do, so that they can see how parents should treat teenagers like themselves.

Bob makes it difficult for anyone to understand him, however. At one minute he gives evidence of admirable qualities of maturity, at the next he lapses into a silliness unbelievable for one of his years. Attacking a difficult responsibility, he performs it "like a man"; yet at some slight infliction of hurt from a chum he flies to parental affection for support like a little boy. In adolescents still bubbles something of the gladness of children; in them also flashes something of the insight of maturity. They are happy combinations of delightful kids and responsible men and women. An adolescent stands

> . . . halfway between childhood, which I have not yet
> put fully off, and
> Manhood, which I have not yet put fully on.
> Therefore, I am a strange mixture of both—
> To the confusion of those who do not know me,
> And the joy of those who do.[1]

No adult can get over into the world of adolescents, once he has left his own adolescence behind. But as a parent or teacher shows himself friend and not judge, young persons will gradually open little doors to their world. Glimpses therein will help that parent or teacher know next time what to say or do—or what *not* to say or do. Probably few make sufficient use of the understandings they already have of adolescents and their world.

2. *Viewing them in terms of the general "developmental tasks"*

common to all growing persons. Each teacher and worker should seek to keep abreast of what is being written by psychologists and sociologists and others pertaining to this strange in-between territory of adolescence. One of the most fruitful approaches is the idea that boys and girls are busily working, consciously and unconsciously, on certain "developmental tasks." Just as a baby is impelled by some inner urgency to kick and stretch and try his voice, so adolescents face certain "jobs" all their own in growing up. Some are farther along than others. Each individual must needs build a self. Intermediates have not progressed as far as seniors; seniors have not progressed as far as older youth. Even adults work at these tasks as long as they live.

One constellation of developmental tasks has to do with understanding and accepting themselves and developing a set of values to live by. Young persons must get used to the physical changes taking place within themselves. They need to learn to accept themselves with their limitations as well as their assets. By learning to understand themselves better, they can the better control themselves.

Another constellation of developmental tasks has to do with their relationships with others. First comes their effort to achieve satisfying relationships with their age mates of both sexes. Theirs is an overwhelming desire to belong. Younger adolescents have natural antipathies to the opposite sex, merging into budding interest; then as growth proceeds, into dating, going steady, and plans for marriage and homemaking. These are years when boy meets girl—years filled with dreams and moonlit nights and senior proms and the first perfume of romance. At summer youth conferences, one of the first questions asked is, "What age should we start going steady?" A popular course is "Friendship and Marriage." After the first timid hesitancy and anti-girl, anti-boy antics of early intermediates, young people become poignantly aware of each other. Having a date for the next school party becomes a symbol of prestige—an emblem of social security or of aching, wistful insecurity. Being left out spells tragedy and young hearts hurt hard.

This innate drive to belong has implications for church work with youth.

49

Friendly acceptance by the group "in the swim" is what these adolescents crave. . . . If an adolescent derives pleasure from association with his clique mates in the church situation, he attends Sunday school, young people's meeting, and church parties. . . .[2]

One of the major jobs before adolescents is that of achieving emancipation from parents and other adults, while maintaining affection. They are beginning to look for security outside of home while "untying mama's apron strings." With their natural desire for freedom, they must learn that with it comes responsibility. They need to develop abilities to choose wisely; to grow in their understanding of parents and of other adults, and to replace rebellion against authority with friendly discussion of issues at stake. During later adolescence, youth seek to become economically independent and to establish themselves as citizens of their world. They need to learn how to function worthily in their homes, their groups, their churches, their clubs, their communities, their larger world.

The greatest of their developmental tasks is that of adventuring in relationships with God. Deeper than all other restlessnesses of adolescents is their need for spiritual anchorage, for a sense of "belonging" with God. Such a centering in God alone gives a sense of personal worth, and provides a point of view for interpreting the universe. Some speak of this task of adolescents as that of "developing a philosophy of life" or "choosing a set of values to live by." Rightness with God gives a cohering center for organizing one's scattered impulses; a focal center for answering questions about the relation of science and religion; a dynamic center for personal spiritual growth.

3. *Viewing them as unique individuals, products of all their yesterdays, with motives and dreams for the future all their own.* "No two young persons are alike, and no one alike any two minutes in succession."[3] A vast range of differences in background may be listed for the individuals in any class or group. These would have to do with:

—Home background (farm, slum, apartmental hotel, trailer, quonset hut, riverboat, bungalow)

50

- —Emotional and physical health (crippled, husky, frail, poised, unstable)
- —Intelligence and aptitudes (mechanical, artistic, leadership potential, studious, scientific)
- —Sex and race (Dubinsky, Smith, Chin, Johnson, Schmidt, Eschinni, Bowen, Dunnagan)
- —Hobbies (gardening, fishing, music, art, reading)
- —Job interests (factory work, professional pursuits, office work, housewife, salesman, doctor, diplomat, scientist)

Some churches are so located that their membership represents largely one economic level, or a roughly homogeneous population. Yet even with an apparently level group of middle-class backgrounds, there may be vast differences as to emotional climate in the homes, cultural interests, and the like.

Add to this the fact that each young person is *feeling his individuality*. No longer is he content to be spoken of as "the Jones' little boy Tommy"; he is now "Thomas J. Jones" in his own right. He demands of his teachers, his club leaders, his parents—in short, of the whole adult world—the right to express *himself*. Perplexing problems occur when youth's assertion of freedom clashes headlong into parents' and others' continuance of authority. A part of the teacher's opportunity is to help each individual recognize himself as unique in the sight of God, a temple to be kept worthy.

To do his work worthily, the church leader needs to know what has gone before in the experiences of these individuals. What have been some of their home influences through childhood? Roots of problems may go deep. What have they been taught through the church during earlier years? What worship helps have they had? What units of study? What recreational events have they enjoyed? In what service projects have they participated? Has their attendance been regular or irregular? What acquaintance with the Bible have they formed to date? Most important of all, what has been the impact of the personalities of their teachers? Those who work with youth and those who work with children should meet often together, to form a "bridge" in their efforts in Christian guidance.

Young persons are feeling their individuality. They ask the right to act from motives all their own. Mary and John sit on the back seat in youth meetings and keep up a whispered conversation during the worship. In the intermediate department, Jimmy keeps nudging the boy next to him, keeping the class in confusion and harassing the teacher. Acts, however, are merely symptoms. What motives prompt such behavior? What inner needs are these individuals attempting to satisfy? Were the needs wrong in themselves, or merely the actions these individuals used for satisfying the needs? Can the worker help them find better channels for expression?

Motives can be appealed to on a low level, or on a higher level. Some workers attempt to force youth's co-operation by building their affections around themselves as teachers. Some put their faith in contests and such like. Young people tend to respond on whatever level they are challenged.

Adult friends can guide young people to see *reasons* for choosing desirable paths of conduct: see them with such clarity and urgency that they will *want* to take the better paths. Thus and thus only do they develop spiritual and moral fiber, the ability to think ahead, weigh consequences, choose wisely. Inner judgment is their need, not outer authority. There will come a time when their teacher will not be by their side to tell them what he thinks. They need a "principle within," as Charles Wesley said; a "way" of living, as Jesus said.

Sam and Susie giggle during a worship service. To be sure, there might not have been an atmosphere conducive to reverence or a well-planned service in the first place. But suppose the service was especially fine. Yet they giggled. One explanation might have been that some friend had hurt their feelings earlier, and they were putting on a bravado act in the group that morning. Or maybe they had been up too late the Saturday night before, and their nerves were overstimulated. Or maybe some flash of spiritual meaning had caused a lump in their throats too big to be held, and finding it necessary to laugh or cry or something—they giggled.

Beckett shattered the quiet of a devotional service in his intermediate department by throwing a hymnal at the central electric light. Motive? Could his counselor have known about his home situation that morning, she might have understood more clearly. Beckett was the youngest in a family of brothers and sisters, all of whom had excelled in some way. At breakfast his mother had bewailed his awkwardness, holding up an older brother as example. Beckett was a bundle of bottled-up frustration. He needed confidence in himself. He was fighting back at the adult world. Eyes lit on the bulb; the hymnal was in hand; he could score a bull's-eye—and he did! Adding to his satisfaction, he became the center of all eyes. What appear to be "discipline" problems are but symptoms. The cause must be found—and it is a holy adventure to help young persons with problems that, left unchecked, may create traumas in personality for life.

4. *Viewing them through the eyes of the Christian faith.* The teacher's eyes, baptized by faith, can see in that redheaded junior high a potential church bishop someday. "This is our faith fantastic." Subtly, by the teacher's own faith in a young person, he helps him square his shoulders and have more faith in himself. The adult friend's belief in him helps him believe in himself. Probably that was the way Jesus coaxed hidden abilities from the motley group of his followers.

Adventure awaits the worker who sets out to grow in his own understanding of young people—baffling adventure, to be sure, at times, but an ever-rewarding one always. Some give up. "These modern youth," they sigh. "Now when I was growing up . . ." Others peg down a few pet notions, but fail to view in fullness youth's growing potentialities. But for those who keep on, delightful discoveries are made, and their work with young people becomes less chore and more privilege. For to observe young persons is to observe God at work. Within each growing life have been implanted "laws of growth," according to a marvelous Plan.

To learn better how to work "with the grain" of the way God made youth is the worker's quest. It becomes a religious experience to observe the miracle of light coming into a boy's face as a new idea dawns on him for the first time; to watch the all-out abandon of seniors performing a task they have set for themselves. Among

53

church workers with youth, there is need for fewer Marthas, cumbered about the "many things" of programs, materials, and the like; and more Marys, who will open their hearts to understand growth as God wills it, and then give of their powers to co-operate. In such humility does the farmer co-operate in growing wheat or the gardener in growing roses.

Achieving Fellowship: Young People and Adult Workers Together

Confidence is a quality adolescents ask in their adult friends in home and church: that those adults closest to them not be muddled, confused themselves. He who is trying so earnestly to achieve self-confidence wants to see examples of it in older personalities. He wants to feel "something solid there." The adult must needs maintain at all times personal integrity.

Confidence in the young person himself is the next need: *willingness* to shift responsibility onto young shoulders and *sensitivity* to know when and how much. No once-for-all ratio as to how much the adult should do and how much expect of the youth can be given. Alertness to the abilities of each young person is the key.

Here is the core of the clash in youth-adult relationships in many churches. This adult has an idea that working with youth means that he "takes the back seat" always. He does just that. His young people *try* to do what is expected; but being younger, they flounder pitifully. They know something is wrong. They are unhappy. Interest in their meetings dwindles. Noise increases. The adult gives up on the grounds that "they're such discipline problems."

Take the opposite extreme. This teacher first began with his group when the members were of junior high age. Now they have reached later adolescence. They are capable of doing much more for themselves now than they could earlier. But unfortunately he was promoted with them, yet his ideas of them have not grown! He still treats them as if they were intermediates. They resent his "domination." Some have left the church.

Let us look a bit more closely at the problem. A vast pageant of growth takes place between the years twelve and twenty-three. One may view this growth somewhat as a river, moving from the com-
54

paratively quiet pools of childhood into the turbulence of early adolescence; on through the less rapid but broader streams of middle adolescence; into the deeper and calmer pools of older youthhood; and on out into the wide waters of adulthood.

The word "adolescence" is too broad for clear meaning. One cannot speak accurately of "characteristics of all adolescents." One cannot begin to think of teaching methods for such a wide age range—for almost opposite methods apply at the two age extremes of junior highs and older youth.

Three distinct stages of growth appear. To be sure, all individuals differ. Growth is uneven and variable. Some mature more rapidly than others. But for the sake of serving the best interests of the largest number, young people should be grouped for church work (Sunday school, evening meetings, any activities) by *stages* of growth. Methods appropriate with each age should be found and used. Thus and thus only can adult friends work "with the grain" of the way God grows youth.

With early adolescents. Workers with this age level will remember how close to childhood they are, no matter how grown-up they would like to think themselves. The adult (in Sunday school, evening meeting, any activity) will assume *major* responsibility in planning ahead all church activities; in collecting resources; in inspiring interest and purpose in these young persons; in helping them choose and plan activities within the scope of abilities and within their brief interest span for completion; in guiding them in accomplishing these plans happily and with a glorious sense of achievement which will be the spur toward attempting one-step-harder tasks next time!

Words that deal with concrete, easily-visualized situations within the experience range of intermediates should be used in all conversation with them. Abstract generalizations are all but meaningless. Discussion must *always* be led by an adult. It cannot proceed for long, because the experience of the intermediates runs out. Activity methods should predominate. Intermediates like and need (have muscle hunger) to move around, make things, do things. They can work in classes and meetings in small committees around small tables, taking pieces of responsibility they can fulfill soon. The worker counsels with them lest they "bite off more than they can chew" and helps them come through with completed plans *of their own.*

Little if any emphasis on office-holding should be made. Youth work generally in America has erred tragically in holding up the idea of getting elected to offices as symbol of prestige, and in guiding youth poorly if at all in ways of achieving healthy, functioning *group fellowship.* Better small short-term committees as needed, perhaps with chairman chosen easily from the group, than slates of officers. Individuals have been known to suffer in their Christian growth while enjoying the overinflation of personal prowess through the spotlighting which elections give, and which adults often unwittingly foster through their urging of individuals to "lead." Committee work that focuses more upon the *job to be done* than upon giving individuals prestige is far healthier for Christian growth.

Early adolescents need wholesome group life in the church where boys and girls learn to think, plan, work, pray, and play together—as foundational fellowship for the time when later they will go together.

Workers will find early adolescents more exuberant and open in their enthusiasms (and in their dislikes) than are senior high or college age youth. Interests are more volatile, shorter-term. They are sampling their world. Hence activities of shorter duration that can be completed during interest spans are advisable.

With middle adolescents. Workers with senior high youth observe that their interests have taken a different turn almost overnight from those predominant with intermediates. These youth are acutely conscious of boy-girl relationships. They can now take more initiative and fulfill more difficult responsibilities. They often "get too many irons in the fire" and sometimes tend to slight their church work.

The discussion method has more value in teaching this age, but high school youth need to be guided by capable, prepared adults who can draw out the shy members and help the total group get somewhere. They tend to skim the surface of questions; to take short cuts; to base decisions on hearsay and prejudice unless firmly guided to sturdier thinking and fact-finding and fact-facing.

Socially, the larger crowd counts, whereas with early adolescents it was the smaller gang. High school youth are easily swayed by group influence. Hence the importance of their keeping the right company, and of having church groups strong enough and attractive enough in their activities to bolster individual idealism.

The adult working with middle adolescents or senior youth is co-planner, friend, resource helper, stand-by-er. There should be mutual interchange of ideas with responsibility gradually shifted to youth shoulders wherever possible. The adult needs to be prepared to offer a variety of possible choices, then let the seniors take their pick. They will be blank when asked, "What would you like to do?" But they will respond readily when given some alternatives from which to choose, or interest finders or check lists to stimulate thought.

High school youth, too, need tactful counseling as they plan. When an individual is to take a church responsibility, he needs friendly coaching, rehearsals behind the scenes, before the meetings. Otherwise he may do his part poorly and lapse into habits of continuing to do so. Slovenly habits in church work too often abound. Youth *can* "give of their best to the Master" and should be challenged to do so!

With later adolescents. These young people are "practically adult." The church worker must realize that their abilities have grown, often beyond his own. Whereas with younger youth he had to take the lead in preplanning, and with middle adolescents he had to "push from behind," now with these older youth he should be able literally to "take a back seat." Occasionally individuals will need special help, particularly personal counseling.

Older youth can be challenged to consider in their classes and meetings the larger issues of world import; to "dig their teeth" into crucial problems of individual and group living as Christians; to think and function effectively as *doers* of the word, and not just talkers. One of the reasons for churches' failure to hold this older group has been their failure to provide activities *sufficiently above the high school level and difficult enough for the growing powers of these youth*. Older adolescents need to be grouped apart from seniors and intermediates. Theirs is a different world.

Thus, the adult worker imagines an upward curve standing for the growing abilities and expanding interests of young people as they move from junior high to senior and to older levels. He visualizes his own ratio of initiative and helpfulness reaching all the way down to where the youngest twelve-year-old starts, then decreasing in exact relation to the increasing powers of the youth.

This permissive relationship, and youth-planning-up-to-the-limit-of-their-capabilities should obtain *whenever* and *wherever* young persons and their adult friends come together—in the home, in the church, in recreation, in worship, anywhere. And let the adult remember that young persons can this week do more than they could last week; and even now can probably do a little more than at first thought the adult imagines!

Achieving Fellowship in Church Groups

More recent studies from psychology, sociology, cultural anthropology and related disciplines, coupled with studies from the educational front affirm that man is far more a "socius" than has formerly been recognized. Potent are the forces playing upon growing personalities, and one becomes a part of all that he has met and all that he has met becomes a part of him. Former writings tended somewhat to deal with adolescents as museum specimens mounted on pins. But to understand young people truly, one must go ever out with them into the social relationships that play such powerful roles in what they are and what they dream of becoming. Much meaning is back of the old rhyme:

> Mother calls me Willie,
> Father calls me Will;
> Teacher calls me William,
> But the fellows call me Bill.

In a sense, each young person puts on a different personality as he goes into each group of which he is a part.

Ralph, growing up on the edge of Chicago's slums, was his Sunday school teacher's pride and joy, for he always knew the most Bible verses. But on weekdays and especially Saturdays, Ralph and his gang pilfered the five-and-dime stores. He was also the pride and joy of his gang for bringing the most loot to the cache.

58

A young person can change like a chameleon—not because he means to be fickle, but because his need for belonging is so great that he will often go to amazing lengths to maintain status in his group. Who knows the personal tragedies of young persons enslaved by drink or narcotics who first began in order for the moment to be "one of the crowd"?

Observe Mary in her church fellowship group. She seems shy, stumbles over her part in the programs, and usually withdraws to a corner during games. She is not sure of herself in this group. But observe her in her Mariners' group. Here she is a vital, confident personality sure of her skill with the boats and sure of her place with the gang.

Not always are such contrasts noticeable. Some young persons tend to withdraw by themselves, rather than trying to make themselves part of a church group. Some have trouble making friends, wistful as they are for companionship. Some ride the crest of waves of popularity. So suggestible are youth generally, that when one starts being popular, others add to his acclaim and put him on the bandwagon. When one seems ignored, the others follow suit and leave him more lonely still. Some individuals sparkle and draw others to them; others form their supporters. Still others hold to the edges. Some make one or two deep friendships and these appear to satisfy. Others need many friends. A young person's happiness and inner well-being is greatly affected by his status with others; and this status is likely to be at different levels in different groups—hence, the differences in characteristics suggested above.

Workers with children and youth in public school, group work and church are learning to note these friendship lines—which way they are tending. In almost every group, a "pattern" will emerge, if the adult observes and keeps notes carefully. A "sociogram" may be drawn, representing each young person by a circle. Some of the circles will be close together, as if drawn by some inner magnet. There are some individuals who are "stars of attraction." An "in-group" will form around them, with friendship-preference lines going in both directions between individuals. The social structure of any group may be diagramed easily by asking individuals to name five especially close friends. Double connecting lines or arrows show mutual friendship; arrows going one way show a friendship not reciprocated.

A little farther from the center of the picture are "fringers," usually with arrows going one-way toward the in-group but not always reciprocated. Still farther away, some with no lines between themselves and others, or lines with only one or two others, are the "isolates."[4] Church workers are urged to be aware of such constellations. To be sure, the diagram itself will not help the situation. But it may reveal to the adult worker where help needs to be given.

A class or group in the church pulsates with human dynamics. Persons can hurt one another—for life; or together, individuals may fuse into a functioning fellowship in which each feels free and at ease to express fearlessly what is in his mind and heart, and in which all together can build. The adult's own pervasive spirit of ease with the young people and genuine enjoyment of them helps set the tone. Young people lack respect for a grown-up who tries feverishly to win their approval and overdoes being a "good fellow." What they ask is plain gingham garden-variety sincerity—the right to be accepted for what they are and to accept the adult for what he is. The first step in achieving healthy fellowship in a church group rests with the adult.

The next step is that of *planning* together constantly, so that activities are the youth's own and not foisted upon them by authority. As noted above, and as will be noted later in connection with units of study, young people must needs have a *purpose* of their own—feel a surging sense of significance in what they are doing. Church work generally has failed to challenge young people—even early adolescents —with sufficiently difficult tasks: real work in a real world! Caught up in an important job of helping somebody in their community, young persons tend to forget themselves and possible individual tensions. They "find themselves" as a group by "losing themselves" in the cause. Group work with youth is far more healthy, mentally, socially, and spiritually, than so much emphasis upon individual work as has been the case with youth work in the past. Committees can bring a richness of ideas to the planning of a unit that one individual

60

"leader" could not. Church work should train young persons in the skills of understanding one another, and in healthy give-and-take rather than in *prima donna* individualism.

Very little organization may be needed in a church department or class or group. As suggested above, overstress on organizational structure and office-holding in the past has perhaps stunted true Christian growth. Some adults may feel insecure without a great structure of youth organization, with offices apportioned out and the "program" to be a "running" of the organization. Their conditioning in the past has been to trust organization too much. *Real* democracy or Christian brotherhood comes from the inside out; it cannot be achieved by scaffolding on the outside. Youth have been known to argue many long hours as to whether the item under consideration was an amendment to the amendment or the previous question. Elections, overemphasis upon parliamentary procedure, and adult stress on "leading" can all drive wedges into the human relationships in a church group—set person over against person, instead of welding all into glad, functioning harmony.

The alternative is for the adult worker to strive more earnestly, carefully, and prayerfully to help young persons *plan* together activities of real worth; then *decide how* to achieve these goals (which achievement may call for different ones taking different responsibilities, possibly electing officers or selecting committees). The *job to be done* should be the center of focus, not the limelight of getting chosen for office or standing up before one's group speaking or "leading." In guiding young persons in worship, emphasis given by the adult should be on *helping the entire group come into fuller fellowship with God* rather than upon the individual standing up front.

Protestant youth work may be at a crossroads now. With the adoption widely of the Five-Commission Plan[5] young people of various denominations may have a bridge of fellowship with one another that they have not had in the past, when each denomination had its separate commission setup. Here at this new crossroads, however, organizational structure may assume an even more gigantic importance; and adult workers may be lulled into thinking that once the Plan of commissions is in operation, they will have less to do.

Rather, theirs will be a far harder task—if the goal be kept in mind of achieving Christian qualities of group fellowship. If with the Plan the attention of youth and their workers can be turned to valiant purposes, plans for achieving them, and ways of *being* Christian in their practice of fellowship, then good. But there is grave danger here of overmagnifying machinery.

Every so often, perhaps, in any church group—from the smallest class in a country church to a big departmental organization—the members and workers should sit down together and ask themselves, "Are we *being* a fellowship? Are we allowing cliques to cause some individuals to feel frozen out? Are we welcoming newcomers and seeing to it that everyone feels thoroughly at ease regardless of the kind of clothes he wears or the kind of car his parents drive? Are we learning to work together thoughtfully, caring more about doing a job well than about who gets the credit, or who gets to go to a conference off somewhere? Do we pass around responsibilities, or tend to spotlight a few outstanding capable ones? Are we drawing in the more timid and shy members and finding activities in which they would be interested and can have the fun of using their talents, too?"

Even younger youth can face squarely their failures to *practice* as church groups, Christian qualities of fellowship. In one department, resentment was expressed over the coming promotion day that would bring in some new younger ones. "We are just now getting going good; we don't want them underfoot." But once they paused and looked at what they were doing in the light of the Christian ideals they discussed in their classes, they decided immediately that their tight exclusiveness of spirit was not worthy. Guided tactfully by the adult worker, they looked through the eyes of the incoming juniors and realized how much these younger ones were looking forward to being in the intermediate department! Enthusiastically, then, they set about planning to make them feel at home; they took names as Big-Brothers, Big-Sisters; planned a party; made visits; took gifts; and worked out an investiture ceremonial.

Church groups should not merely discuss fellowship or brotherhood in the abstract; but should pause occasionally to look at themselves and their practices. Patterns of relationships are not static.

They change, develop, evolve. The adult worker is eager to help them evolve in directions that will enhance Christian growth. The "in-group" can become more and more exclusive, harming those within it as well as those without. The "isolates" can be made to feel more and more lonely. Or more arrows of friendship can point outward as respect for one another grows and as individuals learn better how to appreciate and work with one another. The class or group can itself become a self-satisfied unit ("We like our teacher and want him promoted with us"), or it can be led to reach constantly outward and upward.

A frontier for church work is that of learning better how to help church groups become functioning fellowships, and then how to help these fellowships become redemptive in their influence upon all of society. In stress through the years upon individual salvation, far too little attention has been given to ways groups help or harm both those within and those without. Very little training is given ministers in methods of group work—they learn to preach to the masses on the one hand, or to counsel with individuals on the other. Yet most church work proceeds through small groups.

The sociogram has striking similarity to diagrams of atomic fission. A parable is here. The principle back of fission is that of disintegration, centrifugal forces pulling apart. No defense can be found against disintegration, save one: integration: centripetal forces making for cohesion. Religion, in its root meaning, is a "binding together." The church of the Living God should make for integration: the integration of the conflicting forces within an individual around a dominant center in God; the integration of scattered individuals into cohesive fellowship; the integration of races and nations into brotherhood. The church group of young people, meeting week after week, is a microcosm for proving the integrating power of the Christian religion!

V

WAYS YOUTH LEARN

*Blessed are they which do hunger and thirst after righteousness:
for they shall be filled.* MATTHEW 5:6

We have dared to affirm that church work with young people means
guiding them in the Christian *faith*. This means guiding them to
"love God with heart, soul, strength, and mind; and neighbor as
selves."

How is such a brave goal brought to bear upon what goes on in an
ordinary, average church group of young persons meeting in their
Sunday school class or evening session? Such a goal demands that
young people be guided, not just in thinking or talking about love
for God and neighbor as self, but in actual *practicing, being, becoming, loving.*

There is no such thing as "learning" apart from living, with the
vague idea of "applying" later. Learning is the very stuff of living
and living is the very stuff of learning! We learn what we live and
only what we live. How prepare for loving neighbor on Monday, save
by loving fellow members of one's church group, of one's family,
and of one's other possible relationships on Sunday? The very meeting room for class or fellowship in the church is a "living" room.

There is no teaching where there is no learning. "As soon say
you have sold when no one has bought." "Learning" is a personal
word. Let the word never be thought of as an abstract noun! There
is no such thing as learning apart from persons who learn, who
actively respond, who *change*.

The process is more than a mathematical one, such as the adding
of a specified quantity of knowledge to that already possessed by the
learner. Rather, it is more like a chemical change: different elements
are brought together, a reaction takes place, and the result differs
from what the elements were before. Every hour of every day persons

64

are learning, changing. What stays with them is the imprint of their own reactions to the influences that have been brought to bear upon them. Teachers change, too, because they act and react in the teaching-learning process.

Most changes or learnings in the daily walks of life are small—perhaps so small that for the most part the individual is not conscious of the learning having taken place. He manipulates a tool in a certain way. He finds it does not work so well. He tries a different way, scarcely giving the matter a second's conscious thought. He is *learning*. He is meeting the situation with some reactions all his own, he is finding a solution to a problem that frustrates. One meets larger living situations in a similar way. A significant problem comes upon one's path. Information is needed. One seeks it, sorts it out, relates it to his needs; now, with the facts in, and with his own motives and needs brought to bear upon the situation, one thinks differently. What one has learned is his own thought process of information gathering and decision.

We learn what we live, only what we live, and everything we live. We learn each thing we live as we accept it to act on, and we learn it in the degree that we count it important, and also in the degree that it fits in with what we already know.[1]

A person may not realize consciously the way a succession of small changes is affecting him, until he looks back and notes the cumulative effect or direction his living has taken. Habits are formed; they in turn bring other habits in their train. Like a river fed by small tributaries, general directions of learning become evident.

Sow a thought, reap an act; sow an act, reap a habit; sow a habit, reap a character.

Knowledge alone is not enough—or even the ability to phrase the ideas in the right words. Too much teaching in the past has been informational only. "Much of what we have called religious education has been no more than religious instruction."[2] It has been aimed at bringing facts and having persons agree or memorize or show other evidences of having "learned." But agreeing or even remembering

65

is not enough. It is never enough merely to deal in words. *Doing* is both the method and the test of learning.

A young person may marshal facts until he sees clearly and admits to himself, "This, I believe, would be the more truly Christian way for me to act." But his emotions may get in the way of his intellectual judgment. Emotions are driving forces. What one *wills* to do and *does*—that is what one truly learns. Disobedience to the "heavenly vision" this time makes disobedience or indifference to it easier next time.

The senior class of Oak Grove Church is beginning a study of "The Early Christian Church." For eight sessions or so, they will be surveying some high points of church history, arranging some of the major events in time sequence, discussing implications for heroism today. What will it take, beyond mere exchanging of words, for these seniors to have *learned* something of what the early church brings to them now?

Over in Fairmont, a small village church, the intermediates are getting ready for a coming seven-session unit on "Religion and the World's Work," a prevocational look at some of the workers of the world. The central problem with which they shall be dealing is, "In what vocations can one serve as 'partners' with God?" What will it take for these boys and girls to *learn* something of what working with God means?

In Metropolitan Church in the heart of a big city, the evening fellowship of seniors is approaching its new three-session discussion of "Youth Friendships," discovering secrets of making, finding, and keeping friends while holding on to Christian ideals. What will it take for them to have *learned* what it means to do so?

Church work with youth—Sunday school classes, evening meetings, other activities—often stops too soon, contenting itself with remarks (whether from the lips of the teacher or of young persons in so-called "participation") *about* Jesus' teachings for living. Only as young people, in all classes and meetings (and thus more likely in personal problems in daily living) *practice* making decisions as young Christians, taking stands, and following through, do they *learn* how to do so. How much easier to take it out in talk.

66

How much easier, perhaps, for the teacher to tell them what he considers fitting for young Christians to think and do, than to guide them patiently and perhaps more slowly, to work out conclusions for themselves and consider possible testing times in their living when they will need to draw upon these conclusions. Youth meetings are famous for resolutions-passing. Does their church allow young people at times to lapse into the tempting pseudo-security of having *said*, rather than prodding them until they take the further step into *deed?*

In units of study such as the above, young persons will glimpse a higher line of action in some very specific phase of their living—the more specific the better, for Christianity must be given "traction" in the wear and tear of daily life. Let these young people, once they have determined clearly their Christian ideal, pause to preview some possible temptations that may face them. They know, probably better than their teacher, what these temptations may be. Let them come to grips. Are they, or are they not, ready to face these choices? Let them pray. God meets the heart in the throes of decision-making. In Him, and only through Him, are resources for holding true.

In the hearts of human beings everywhere are slumbering potentialities for greater God-companionship, for more thoroughly God-centered lives. Yet somehow the teaching that goes on in the churches often falls short of awakening these potentialities! In the people are possibilities for fellow-feeling with others, for responding heroically. Let them be touched while young with the Christian dynamic. All work with youth in the church, each unit, each activity, each plan is "for a verdict"!

Materials Are Provided

The teacher or counselor of young people, responsible for meeting with them in the Sunday church school or evening meeting, asks, "How can I know what my young people need most to learn for their Christian growth?" "Are there some leads as to what Bible and other materials will help them, at their stage of growth?" "Is there something that gives me clues as to methods for working with them?"

The answer is in the printed curriculum materials made available denominationally and interdenominationally for young people themselves and for adults who work with them, whether in the Sunday church school class or evening meeting or in other contacts. There are reading books, attractive quarterlies, and other types of guides for use by the intermediates, seniors, or older youth themselves and addressed directly and appealingly to that age level. There are teachers' and counselors' helps, and increasingly in some of the denominations, parents' helps as well.

Denominational curricula are planned systematically in "cycles" for each age level from earliest childhood through adulthood. The guidance materials for intermediates (ages 12-14 or in junior high school), for seniors (ages 15-17 or in senior high school), and for older youth (ages 18-23 or college and career) build upon what came before in earlier years and build toward what will come later. That which is found when Mrs. Z opens her printed helps to prepare for the next unit is no hit-or-miss matter. This unit is a part of a carefully planned system; it is the only one of its kind; if she omits it, the young people will lack for the specific helps it contained. It fits into a scheme whereby the basic idea as introduced in earlier years is now amplified, and later further and fuller guidance will appear.

During the years when they are early adolescents, young persons need help especially on specific problems of living, of getting acquainted with their larger world and with their own new selves. Their mental and spiritual development is such as to enable them to comprehend and use certain Biblical materials particularly meaningfully. Certain aspects of church history may have fresh and vigorous appeal at this age. Biography can usher into their own aspirations some new heroic ideals.

Later, when they have grown to the senior-high stage, they will have changed their interests markedly. Now a whole new range of problems has come upon them. Furthermore, their mental and physical development, and potentially their spiritual development, has progressed amazingly. They can—and should—now venture more deeply into certain Christian truths. They can grapple more deeply with problems through discussion. They can undertake harder tasks of service. In a few years they will have grown into later adolescence —when they can move out still further on Christian truths, use their Bibles more understandingly, enlarge their perspectives, and spread their scope of service action and giving.

Thus, the growth cycle of young persons is the key. Workers in a local church who fail to provide these graded materials, keyed to each age level and no less keyed to the centralities of the Christian faith and the Bible, are thereby robbing their youth of helps they need at just those stages of present development! They are shutting out guidance that will make Christianity and the Bible come alive, in the thought forms—possibly in the living—of these teen years now.

Materials Are Offered in Units

When one looks at the bigness of a young person's need, he becomes frightened at its enormity. How dare to be a teacher of youth in such a time? But if a small "piece of experience" is taken at a time, the young people can be helped step by step—"first the blade, then the ear, then the full corn in the ear." These smaller "pieces of experience" along the Christian way may be called "units." Denominational and interdenominational curricula offer such "units," in delightful variety but all fitting together in a carefully wrought structure that meets needs for Christian growth at each age level.

Each "unit" represents a possible *journey of growth* for the young persons themselves—from where they now are to what they may become, with the help of the ideas in the unit, the teacher, and the Living Christ. Each unit presupposes action, movement by the young persons themselves. No one else can take the journey for them.

Units in the printed helps will be found to be of differing lengths. Why? Because some areas are bigger than others, more important for their Christian development. It will take longer to work through on one problem than another. Units are more than mechanical slices of subject matter. They are maps for a journey.

The editors and lesson writers who have prepared these printed unit materials have sought to imagine just where this age group

69

of youth would likely be, in their attitudes and understandings on the subjects at hand. They have asked, "At just what point would young persons of this age naturally *begin* if they wished to get somewhere on this subject?" "What first steps would be necessary?" "Where would each step lead?" "How long would it probably take the average group to reach meaningful conclusions?"

Thus a "unit" is shaped up and the printed resource materials are made ready to put into the hands of the teacher or counselor and of the young people themselves. Here are aids for the journey, pointing out the goal, some paths leading toward it, and possible explorations along the way. The editors have not merely taken scissors and clipped off segments of Christian doctrine, Bible, and the like, and in turn cut these into Sunday session topics. Rather, they have sought to picture young people and their needs, and to provide both incentive and helps for their journeys—over into the land of fuller, more abundant Christian living.

A Journey the Young People Take for Themselves

The adult worker, whether Sunday school teacher or counselor for evening session, needs a mental picture of this "journey of experience" with young persons starting where they now are and moving step by step toward higher ground. This is a different proposition, in terms of the preparation the adult needs to make, from getting a lecture ready. His purpose and plans are geared to helping young persons *see* possibilities farther on, *want* to move, *decide* and *take steps for* themselves, and—to some extent at least—*arrive,* and *look back* over how far they have come. This process of moving involves young people on all cylinders—in their thinking, feeling, willing, doing.

Implications are obvious. In the Sunday church school, if the worker's habits have been to "get up a lesson at a time," or to regard teaching as largely meaning telling, or to think he can wait until Saturday night to begin to prepare . . . such habits will have to be left by the wayside. In Sunday evening sessions, if committees of young people or individuals have been accustomed to last-minute (if any) preparation, or to "reading parts" in meeting, or to regard

70

their materials as merely "programs" to be put on . . . such habits will have to be left by the wayside.

For *both* the Sunday morning and Sunday evening units, *both* the adult worker and planning committees of young people need to review what is meant by "learning," start with basic principles, visualize the possible unit journey a given unit offers, and prepare throughout by *units-at-a-time*, not mere isolated Sunday lessons with no apparent relation to what went before or what will come after. It is necessary for them to have the full material for the entire unit as they begin, if at all possible. Increasingly, denominational houses are making full units available, to encourage better planning. The planning is somewhat like taking a road map and penciling in possible destination (the purpose of the unit), and roads leading there (steps).

First the adult worker makes general over-all preparation (see later chapter for summary in detail of steps he takes); then, meeting with committees of young people, he and they scan the unit material; decide upon clear, definite purposes, with the youth secretary making notes of just what these purposes are; map out tentative step-by-step plans; suffuse the planning with prayer; arrange the room, equipment, and needed materials; and *believe* powerfully that through this very unit something dynamic, something life-changing may take place!

Any dates that appear with printed helps need not be taken as literal commands that all groups be ready for or finish with certain materials by a certain time. A better plan is to take the time span of an entire unit as boundaries for the time budget; then worker with youth committee can roughly decide just what will be the best steps for *them*, so as to complete and round out the process if possible in the time suggested for the unit as a whole. Some groups will take longer to "warm up"; others may work at faster pace. By all means plenty of time for summarizing near the close of the unit should be allowed, charted into the time budget. Then both worker and group can work along steadily and without rush.

As suggested elsewhere, it is highly advisable for youth councils to appoint planning committees to work with teachers for the

71

Sunday school units, just as such committees work with counselors for their evening session units. There is no valid reason why "youth participation" should be limited to evenings. The important thing is to get at *how youth best learn,* any time, any place.

The adult worker who plans with committees by *units* (rather than merely a Sunday at a time) will feel the inner urgency of being present with his group at every step—else he will not know where they are. For a teacher to drop out without good reason for one Sunday during a unit leaves the young people in a difficult position; and no substitute who has not shared the process from the initial planning can come into a unit journey. If a worker knows ahead that he will have to be absent for a Sunday, he should have an assistant with him from the first step of planning. (A good idea, anyway!)

The experience of planning and working through units may hold answer to oft-heard criticisms that "young people these days do not know what they believe." If, before leaving a certain unit, the youth themselves put into their own words just what they have learned and what they feel they should do about this—then they will be able to put into words their growing convictions for outsiders. Each unit marks a convenient milestone. Both the young people and their leaders can pause there to say, "Thus far we have come." There is a glow of achievement, unit by unit; and an over-all sense of making progress in chosen directions. In itself, this achievement is productive of regular attendance.

Long-Range Planning

Youth groups, even those of early teen years, will enjoy taking time once in a while during their church year, to stop and think what their interests and questions are. Check lists or interest finders may be used; or the members may simply speak up in forum style while someone lists their suggestions on board or paper. Question boxes are useful.

In some churches, each age group takes a fall retreat (possibly for a day camp, or over a week end at a camping spot) to plan ahead tentatively some of its main emphases for the year. Not only do young persons grow through the direct experience of planning

72

immediate units, but they gain much from looking ahead and learning to do long-range planning as well. To be sure, the younger intermediates and seniors will need much adult help and counsel, but they can share in such a process and their contributions will be original, sincere, helpful.

Value, then, is not only in the rich variety of good thoughts they bring out which will make their program stronger; value is also in the young persons themselves as they are helped to pause and crystallize a little more clearly in their own minds what they *do* need and wonder about and worry about in matters religious. For many, unless they have such opportunities, religion is a vague blur. Finer psychological attitudes will obtain toward the units coming later if the young people first list such areas from a sense of their own felt need.

Once a goodly coverage of interests and needs is obtained, then the committees can look over the denominational yearbooks showing what unit titles will appear for Sunday school and evening meeting for the particular age level. Some denominations offer, in addition to *dated* curriculum units, undated pamphlet electives which can be used at any time during the year when interest and need calls for attention to that problem. It can almost be guaranteed that almost all subjects a given age level would raise will be found approached in some way in the year's list of units, or at least the cycle's (three-year period) list. A good plan is to build a calendar—perhaps in four sections, one for each three-month period for morning and evening; or perhaps in a long scroll of wrapping paper with the months drawn off (possibly even illustrated artistically!).

The units dealing with those areas in which keenest interest has been expressed will be charted in first; and if there is no particular reason for *not* putting them in on the dates they appear in the curriculum, let those months be used. A wise plan for the most part is to follow rather closely the dated units for the Sunday church school sessions in the mornings—these are usually the big solid red-meat units of the Christian faith; then there may be more leeway for rearrangement, use of undated pamphlet electives, and further choice for evening sessions. Each year's offering of units for morning and evening gives excellent "vitamin" balance; but adult workers should look also at the *cycle,* for a unit with a particular desired slant not appearing in the current year might have been in the last quarter of the year just preceding, or may come soon in the year following. Workers who tend to pick up just one quarter's material and shake their heads in solemn judgment are warned that they are not getting thus a full picture. Not all dishes that are good for young people can be placed on their table for any one meal.

What happens when a teacher decides to throw aside the denominational curriculum and "shop around" or "use the Bible only" or "have outside speakers"? He is *robbing* his young people of this careful cycle plan of spiritual vitamins. Perhaps some units he omits will never come again and they will grow up without the specific helps these units offered.

Further, in his mistaken zeal for Bible teaching, he may be robbing his young people of the best in Biblical scholarship and interpretation, breadth and variety of Scripture selections, and helpful insights for the present day. Denominational houses spend thousands assembling the finest in Biblical scholarship and in good teaching methods. A local worker—who, the chances are, has not had particularly extensive training in Bible, and who, the chances are, does not have very much extra time to spend in preparation—sets himself up as authority when he throws away helps in favor of teaching the Bible. Unwittingly, he is defeating his own goal.

Nor do adult workers with youth in a church have full right to throw out or leave in without letting the young people *themselves* share in planning. To be sure, youth cannot do the whole job of selecting their spiritual menus, particularly during younger years; they themselves respect the fact that their church offers them a rich, full variety of helps for their growth and *stirs* dormant interests to life. Sometimes young people need to be awakened to some need they have not yet faced; they need to have their appreciations and sympathies broadened in ways they cannot now say. All this will happen as they go along. But if constantly, throughout the church year, the youth in fellowship with their workers think and plan, the chances for fuller youth interest and attendance are far greater!

A value of having their calendar of chosen units for morning and evening out before them (maybe on the wall or at least quickly accessible) is that they can chart in related activities of recreation, special service action plans, celebration of festivals—in short, they can see their "program" whole, branching out from the units as the life-giving stem of the vine. (One reason why youth "programs" are lifeless in many churches is that they fail to do this long-range planning of their *units*. They try to build a "program" on organizational activities only, starting with commissions and such like. These are like branches, but without the life-nurturing stem supplying motivation for activities in commission and such areas, these are like branches amputated.)

Problems About Materials

1. *No printed materials can make up for the adult worker's lack of preparation, or failure to use good methods.* Materials are inanimate. They cannot talk back. One can excuse himself by saying, "The writer of this material did not know groups like mine."

The chances are that the writers *have* faced similar problems, else they would not have been asked to write. No writer can have in mind the needs in all types of churches. Mrs. Young at Cosmopolitan Church in Big City, and Mr. Olds at Bethel Church in Possum Hollow must be the "bridge" between the printed materials and their young people. As teachers, they clasp hands with the lesson writer on the one side and with a young person on the other.

Occasionally a request will come into a denominational publishing house, "Please send me materials I will not have to prepare." Such is a confession of low rating of youth, the teaching task, and the Christian cause. Where a worker scorns the fine suggestions in the teachers' helps because he does not wish to be bothered trying to get ready for a new activity, is he not purchasing his own security in his old methods at a possible price of youth's interest? Where he "tells" instead of preparing to help them find answers for themselves, is he not choosing the easier way for himself at the expense of their richer, deeper learning? Materials can help by making clear some possible *purposes* for a unit journey, some 1-2-3 pathways.

But young people with their worker must see and choose and do. No press has been invented that turns out materials already read. No printed helps can "pre-fabricate" the worker's preparation.

2. *Churches may expect difficulties when the recommended materials are not ordered to match the age levels of the youth.* A complaint sometimes heard is, "These evening materials are 'over the heads' of my group." It may be found that in this group where senior-older youth materials are being ordered, over half are intermediates. Materials are available for *each* age level. Workers should *specify* exactly what they wish, and how many copies. In some churches mistakes in ordering go on for years; dollars are wasted; young lives suffer. It is the youth worker's mainline job to *know* first of all what is best for his age level, and to see to it that the right helps are ordered and the teachers' and counselors' notes to match. For years in one church the helps for one age were ordered with pupils' materials for another; workers found it easier to blame the editors than to investigate the difficulty.

3. *Materials should be offered in accordance with youth's own expressions of need and interest when possible, and not alone by decisions of adults.* Unwittingly, adults tend to think of what *they* like; what appeals to *them*. But they are at a different stage of the life cycle. A teacher says, "I didn't like the intermediate materials; I liked the uniform better, so I started using it with my class." The uniform outlines based on adult categories of experience would perhaps appeal more to the adult mind.

4. *Undated elective units may help answer special needs.* "My seniors wanted to discuss boy and girl friendships, so we dropped our church materials and brought in outside speakers." Yet in the forthcoming units and in undated electives were some excellent helps keyed to just such needs. "My class wanted to find out more about the Bible," says a worker vaguely. "So we just put aside our lesson quarterlies." Yet in the dated and undated helps were carefully-prepared introductions to the use of the Bible, interpretations of its different sections. That worker—and there are many like him—may have *closed* a door (possibly to stay closed forever) by denying his group the benefits of these aids geared to their very own age level.

76

5. *Bible permeates the recommended graded materials for each age level.* Whether the word "Bible" appears in the title of a certain piece of material or not, workers can rest secure in the knowledge that curricula are shot through with Bible: (1) in direct Bible study, or (2) with units based on Bible teaching as it applies to life. There is far more *quantity* of Bible offered in the graded cycles than in lessons based on uniform texts selected for adults. A lesson does not have to have large sections of Scripture printed at the beginning in bold type to be Biblical. (Why reprint sections thus save for situations where even the teacher forgets to bring a Bible.) The adult worker and the young people are all supposed to have Bibles or have access to them for looking up references.

Study of the graded curricula for each age level reveals a well-rounded approach to the Bible, with each year's materials building upon what went before. The provision for such a wide range of methods in using the Bible helps keep interest high so that young people will continue to adventure with their Bibles.

a. For each unit, and for each lesson within a unit, there are definite Scripture references. A listing for the year will reveal wide "coverage."

b. All units, whether starting directly with Bible, or starting with problems of living (as Jesus started in His teaching), contain abundant references to other parts of the Bible, *in addition* to the "Scripture lessons" for those units.

c. In every three-year cycle of units, a large number of direct Bible units are included—thus offering a systematic study of the Bible through the years: a knowledge of its content and skills for using it.

d. Vacation school units, and materials for weekday religious education, summer camps and conferences all have Scripture references, and many offer direct Bible study. These, too, are keyed to the age levels of youth.

The less a person knows about the Bible, the less he recognizes it in the lesson materials! There is in every unit a wealth of Bible material: explanations, allusions, references, interpretations.

Many criticisms regarding the amount of Bible in the church school curricula are made after a quick surface glancing through the pages of one quarterly: a quantitative look rather than a qualitative look. One saying from the mouth of Jesus, as recorded in one of the gospels, may have more dynamic for living than vast sections of historical material, for example.

Youth's teachers are concerned with more than mere amount of words about the Word: that their young people become doers . . .

6. *Units offer a variety of suggestions as to methods, among which the workers and youth committees may choose.* "We stopped using our denominational units," complains a worker, "because there was more material than we could get over." The adult worker's function is to choose and guide his young people in choosing so that the important Big Ideas in the units are thoroughly considered. Teaching is more than "getting over the materials" or "covering" lessons. Meanings need to be uncovered! Suggestions as to the *how* should be studied as carefully by the worker as suggestions on the *what* or the content of the units. One is teaching young people, not units.

When a teacher places himself imaginatively in the shoes of the young persons themselves, he begins to see more as they see. Like Ezekiel he should be able to say, "I sat where they sat." The teacher will understand how younger youth, particularly, get tired of sitting! They want to move about. They want to find answers, not merely be told. They want to do—at least, they will if they see a purpose that seems sufficiently significant to them. When they see a point or have an idea, they'll feel, "Please, Mr. Teacher, don't beat me to the point and tell the answer first—I want to find it and say it myself!"

A worker may demur, "But we have so little time in our sessions and I must hurry and tell them, to be sure they get something." Actually, in most churches, the time can be far more carefully shepherded. But the fewer the number of minutes available, the more urgently do the youth need the chance to learn through their own doing. If telling is one of the least effective methods of teaching, then should it not be the last method turned to when time is at a premium? Far from being a short cut to learning, it may be the longer way 'round. The real danger is that it may fool the teacher into thinking a lesson has been learned because words have been said.

When time is short, better that the worker select the most important aspect of the lesson or unit, the very heart of it; keep central focus there; and in the time available, lead the young people in working through that idea for themselves in as direct and rich a way as possible.

The importance of keeping in mind the learner's point of view applies no less to Sunday evening sessions than to Sunday school class sessions. The adult worker in each case is concerned that the young people be helped in the maximum way possible to grow as Christians. If the experience of educators, coupled with hard common sense, suggests that persons learn best through setting up purposes of their own and working actively for the achievement of these purposes, should such methods be confined to any one session, morning or evening? Does the clock have anything to do with method?

A glance back into the history of the Sunday school and youth organizations will reveal first the extreme situation where adult teachers sought (with the best of spiritual intentions) to guide, tell, or otherwise influence young persons into learning Bible truths. This "pattern" became associated with the Sunday school period. But many youth rebelled at what appeared to them "adult domination." They must have their *own* meeting, hold office, carry on activities, choose their own topics, participate! Thus an extreme of youth-do-it all arose in connection with evening sessions. But in this latter, as in the former, youth may not be learning Christian practices—they may learn to do church work poorly, they may flounder with topics far too great for their experience or abilities to decide without help.

Clear thinking suggests rather an attempt on the part of adult workers with youth, whatever their time of meeting, to understand basic principles by which learning is enhanced. Some may object, "But how then have *variety* as between morning and evening sessions?" In the first place, variety is not to be sought merely as an end in itself. In the second, it will come naturally because *each unit* (whether morning or evening) will call for some special kinds of activity, different from those called for by other units. Let workers then note carefully the helps on *methods* as well as on content.

7. *The teacher's own attitudes about materials are contagious.* One says, "I showed my group this material; they shrugged their shoulders." Did the worker impart his own attitude through tone of voice? Youth are responsive.

8. *Thoughtful preparation with good materials and good methods will help answer questions about "discipline."* Once interest is captured and young abilities are focused on something significant to them, "discipline" problems will probably not arise. Real "discipline" must always come from the inside; it cannot be put over from the outside. Has the worker perhaps confused quietness and apathy with "behaving"? In a group, small committees may meet in corners, each carrying on animated conversation and using materials. To an outsider walking in, the room may resemble a shambles; and the hubbub may sound deafening. Here, however, is "creative chaos." Each little work group has purpose. In ten minutes the chairs will be drawn back into the central circle; representatives of each group will tell what was decided; the group as a whole will discuss.

All a young person needs is to get caught up in the significance of the job being worked out; he will cease to be a problem, either to himself or to his group. He "finds" himself by "losing" himself. "Character," it has been said, "is the by-product of a worthy cause made personal." The adult's opportunity all along the way is to expose young lives continuously to worthy Christian causes . . .

"Freedom" is never synonymous with absence of control. Youth freedom can grow as "disciplines" (sense of inner responsibility for getting jobs done, willingness to help one another, brisk application and careful use of time) grow *within* the youth. The adult's goal is diminishing outward control or absence of bending youth to his purposes, and increasing self-control and freedom on the part of the young persons themselves.

Teacher, worker, parent, pastor become friendly helpers, not dominators or dictators. The younger youth will naturally require more help than will older youth. But in all contacts with young lives, whether in the role of teacher in the Sunday school or counselor

80

in the evening meeting or whatever, the adult is more like the ideal *coach*—showing the young people the plays, helping them develop skills, stimulating them to do their best, but never robbing them of *their own right to carry the ball*. For they must be the ones to learn to carry it, each in his own game of life.

VI

SOME TYPES OF UNITS FOR LEARNING

The Spirit itself beareth witness with our spirit, that we are the children of God. ROMANS 8:16

Life is made up of different types of experiences. Sometimes it moves along like a quiet stream, until suddenly a difficulty is encountered. Rocks ahead! A problem to be solved.

After the rapids may come a quieter stretch. But the stream is growing, fed by many small brooklets. It is absorbing much it will carry along.

Sometimes there is a wider spot where the waters spread and wait, reflecting in their depth the beauty of sky and scene. Not tarrying, but waiting.

Just so, life requires of everyone problems to be solved, information to be absorbed and carried along, and times of quiet reflection.

Young lives need these three major types of experiences. Therefore, in their church guidance in Sunday school, evening fellowships, and the like, there should be these three major types of experiences. At times the need will be for grappling with a problem and seeking a workable solution in harmony with Christian principles as they are understood. At other times the need will be for gathering information and relating it to problems of living. At still other times the need will be for quiet opening of hearts to the wonder and mystery, the beauty and the greatness of God, His world, His people, and His way.

We have seen how the curriculum for a given age level of young people (including Sunday school and evening meeting) offers helps on a full range of subjects. Now, we discover that viewing curriculum from the standpoint of subjects is not enough. We see it also in terms of the *kinds of experiences* the youth need to have, in working each of these units out. "Bible" may be a subject. What will be the approach? Depending on the age level and its abilities, their interest at the particular time, and their need for full-rounded Christian growth, the approach in a Bible unit may be: the taking up of a specific Biblical problem to be thought through; the gathering of information needed for their own purposes; the opportunity for awakening to deeper meanings through quiet meditation.

1. *Units of the curriculum leading young people to problem-solving experiences.* For younger boys and girls or junior highs, there are fewer units of this nature; for seniors and older youth, more. The units for each age level will begin "where the young people are": that is, with problems felt within their own experience range. Older youth, and to some extent seniors, are becoming increasingly concerned with problems in the larger community and world. Young people at each stage of growth have personal, immediate problems but the crux of these problems varies markedly from age to age. For this reason, the ages need to be separated at every situation possible, even in the smaller churches, with at least class groupings of their own.

There are fewer problem units in the denominational curricula than units of the other types; young people must not be overloaded with problems they cannot cope with until they develop defeatism. Usually, a unit with a problem to be solved will follow a good meaty unit on resources for Christian thinking, decision-making, and action.

Such a unit focuses on one problem, as its core. The printed helps for the young people confront them with the problem; help them feel its pinch; guide them to want to find a solution; and suggest significant considerations about the Christian way as criteria for deciding. There may be thought-provoking questions probing into the problem and helping them feel it is *theirs.* Some ideas others have found may be included. Queries may lead the young people to think through aspects they might not otherwise consider. There may be suggestions for prayer, that the young people seek guidance from Above and not only from the aid of others, the printed resources, and their adult leader.

Some problems will be felt keenly by young people already. "That bothers me." "I'm puzzled about this." Other problems, being farther perhaps from their immediate awareness, may need to be brought into closer range by the adult worker. How? Visual helps, perhaps;

or stories well told; or resource persons who themselves have had firsthand touch with such problems. Faraway problems should be brought near, as with distant scenes through a telephoto lens.

Adult workers make a grave mistake if they begin imparting information or suggesting *their* solutions *before the young people have first been led to feel the grip of the problem for themselves*. They must see it, feel it, and want to solve it. Until *they* have purpose, they will not care to think through to solutions, much less commit themselves. But until young people are led to grapple with matters of sin and evil in their own lives and in the world, to consider ways of overcoming barriers and creating more Christian communities, they are not having a full-orbed experience of "learning." For real learning-teaching is evangelistic. It calls for decision-making; to launching forth bravely whatever the cost, for Christ's sake.

2. *Units leading to the gathering and interpreting of information.* Such units abound in helpful facts—sometimes too many facts for the amount of curiosity a young person may have at the time! "History of the Christian Church," "The Story of the Hebrew People," or "Paul the Dauntless" may seem far away from his immediate problems or enthusiasms.

The adult worker's task is to awaken the young people first to a sense of *need*. Their native curiosity may be piqued. Their sense of adventure may be kindled. They must have a *purpose* (as definite and as specific as in the case of a problem to be solved) before they will pursue the knowledge which the unit material contains in such glorious abundance. They must be conscious of some *uses* for the information. This fact about the nature of young persons bares the fallacy of the old method of "teaching a lesson, then 'applying' it." The order is backward. Until a young person sees some "application"—some significance he feels is tremendously important for his own life—he will not have motive for mastering the information the unit offers.

Procedure, then, is *not* to begin by "dishing out" some dry pablum of information in the opening session of a Sunday school or evening unit. Rather, a necessary first step is to find what interests of these boys and girls already lie close to this area. How awaken their curiosity? How lead them to realize that they *need* to know about this

84

particular topic? Suppose such a process of soil-stirring consumes the entire first session or longer, thus throwing the remainder of the unit behind in the dates listed in the materials. Little matter. There will be no teaching until the young people are ready to learn.

The next step is *not* for the adult worker (or for youth participants) to "tell" the answers to the rest of the group. That way of doing robs the youth of the zest of exploring and discovering—just when they are about to come upon some new truth, or some intriguing idea, or some important fact. Rather, once they see what it is they want to find out, they may plan ways of doing so, working in committees or as individuals. Some may make interviews. Some may find what the printed helps suggest on the idea. Some may find pictures or other aids to help. Sometimes they may gather helps during the week; sometimes they may divide into little work groups during the regular session time at the church. Suppose there is a little class of six in a small church; would not such procedures be as easy and meaningful for them as for a large group in a larger church? Suppose the time is limited; should not the teacher then quickly tell the answers? No! The more limited the time, the more urgent the need for young people to discover for themselves. They learn in an hour or in a minute only by purposeful doing for themselves. They will gain more through their own activity in dealing with one small segment of the unit, than through having an adult skim the surface of much material through abstract words and ideas they are not ready to assimilate.

3. *Units bidding for deepening appreciations and sympathies.* There will be a number of units in denominational curricula, particularly for younger youth, appealing to the emotions, awakening sympathies, deepening appreciations, stirring purposes. Units rich in biography or colorful with stories from mission fields are examples. *Time* and unhurriedness are essential. The stream that is not quiet cannot reflect. Such appreciational experiences go deep into life, and often supply motivation for fuller Christian living. Likewise, they provide foundation for later problem-tackling. Too often, young persons (adults, too) are asked to work on problems in areas in which they have not yet developed a fund of appreciational insight. In the area of race relations, for example, they need first to have their

85

spirits warmed into appreciation of the vast contributions made by different racial and ethnic groups. Such orientation is emotional, not alone coldly intellectual. It calls forth sympathy and empathy. Only by being guided into many such appreciational experiences will young people have a wealth of inner resources (or know where to find and use such outer resources) for doing straight thinking about problems.

To be sure, within a given unit there may be provision for all three basic types of experiencing. However, most units have a "key" pattern, often obvious in the very title or immediately apparent as a worker begins to prepare. Here is one that opens up a problem; but as a step toward its solution, some further information will be needed. Committees of young people working with their adult leaders will quickly learn to recognize "key" types of experiences needed; and when they do, they are on the road to plan—not merely in old ways of dealing first with subject matter and figuring how to make it palatable—but in ways that will lead to deeper levels of inner awareness and conviction on the part of the learners.

Young People With Their Workers Choose Pathways of Learning Appropriate

There is nothing mysterious about good teaching-learning "methods." The common sense principle is simply the turning to those paths that lead most naturally and obviously in the direction of the goals the group has chosen for its particular unit journey. There is no such thing as "activity method" or "project method" as such. When young people are active—along hundreds of possible lines— they are having *activity;* if they are projecting ideas and plans forward and striving to carry them out, they are having a *project.* The crucial question is, What is their *purpose* at the given time for the immediate kind of activity? As Christian teachers and workers, we dare not take as our purpose simply getting them active, or working on projects. Our concern must go much deeper. How awaken the young people to *want* to reach a goal? Then, how help them choose exactly what paths will best lead them there? The activity should seem *inevitable* for a group's unit journey at a certain stage, not something extra as a sideline. One activity may be needed in a certain unit, but be highly inappropriate in another. The group's own need is determinative.

One teacher became excited about simulated stained-glass windows. She observed another teacher using this "method." Soon her young people were making windows with every unit that came along, regardless of the type of experience the unit called for. Role-playing is an idea that some teachers, seeking to be abreast of the very latest, may be in danger of overdoing, or wearing thin from inappropriate use. Arising through the Moreno brothers' creative efforts in their "theater of spontaneity," psycho-drama (for therapy purposes) and socio-drama (for more informal approach to social problem situations) are of dynamic possibilities. For long years, church groups particularly with intermediates have used impromptu drama, creatively and spontaneously worked out around gripping ideas, or around life in Bible times, or around scenes in church history or on the mission field. Role-playing as originally evolved is a somewhat different matter in that it presupposes a personally felt problem in human relationships, and one attempts to step into the "role" of the person toward whom one feels tension. Careful thinking will suggest what *types* of drama, then, belong with different kinds of units—whether the narrative type depicting in a colorful way scenes otherwise far away in time or space; or whether the deep-searching type opening up problems in relationships. Role-playing, because of its tremendous emotional freight, can have dangerous possibilities unless carefully used. No one method should be used just because it is an attractive method in itself.

Common sense and a little practice, on the part of youth planning committees and adult workers, will indicate what is appropriate and helpful. The making of simulated windows might be an especially helpful procedure in a unit on "Beauty in Our Church Heritage." But for a problem-solving unit on youth friendships, its inappropriateness is apparent. And the teacher who attempted to use role-playing in a unit on the sacraments was perhaps letting a method get in the way of helping her young people think earnestly of deeper meanings to themselves of the worship experience . . . that can never be acted out without sacrilege but must spring sincerely from the heart.

Some workers with youth have a "discussion complex." A teacher complains that her group sometimes shut up like clams. They should at times when there is no *need* for discussing (when there is no controversial issue or no differing points of view). The value of any activity (or "method" of teaching-learning) depends upon the young person's own purposes. Repetition in and of itself may be of little value except in a technical way unless the young person has purpose in the repeating. The boy kept after school to write "I have *gone*" one hundred times (presumably in order to learn the correct verb form) wrote a note for the teacher, "Teacher, I have went home now." *His* purpose had no doubt been to do what teacher said and get it over as soon as possible. We learn our reactions.

We learn each thing we live as we accept it to act on, and we learn it in the degree that we count it important. . . .[1]

The learner's purpose may be set at a lower level or a higher. Is "please teacher" the highest possible level? "Say what we think she wants us to say?" "Get up and perform and have the group think us wonderful?" Some church activities with youth would appear to be aiming only at lower levels as to youth purposes.

Some activities lack the element of *challenge*. A worker with young people in Sunday school or evening meeting may propose too-easy or inconsequential activities, if he is trying to use activity for activity's sake. Young people have the right to choose to spend their time and energies on activities that *matter*. Those activities that call for thoroughgoing probing into a problem, hard and difference-making efforts to improve community evils or to serve others in need—those are the activities that awaken young people to the thrill in the Christian religion! They must "go by way of the cross" from where they now are to a higher level of living!

Too much emphasis—far too much—has been placed by well-meaning workers upon "youth participation" as an end. A young person learns his own reactions. As he "takes part" is he learning to love the limelight? To concentrate on his own performance as "star"? To make slipshod preparation because he knows little is expected, or because earlier he was praised by teacher for what he knew to be too little effort?

Take, however, a group preparing to use a portion of the Scriptures in a choral reading as a part of a period of worship. How quickly and easily they will memorize, almost without realizing they are doing so, for theirs is high purpose: to help the others, through bringing out the great meanings of these Scriptural thoughts, to worship God better. Upon the quality of their purpose depends the value of their activity for the young people themselves and for the others they touch.

Emphasis, then, for youth themselves and for their workers, is not upon product so much as upon purpose and process—what is happening inside the young persons.

A worker hears that "writing a litany" is a good idea. He hurries home to try it with his group. He fails, however, to stir the soil before planting the idea. His young people do not respond. He discounts the whole litany idea. "Won't work with my group," he concludes. Was he perchance thinking first of the external *product* (the finished litany) more than the *purpose* his young people might have in composing one and the *process* by which they might be led to do so sincerely—for a litany is a prayer and not just an "activity." How help them feel such thankfulness for God's good gifts that they crave a way for gathering together some of their many upsurging prayer thoughts? The actual form, whether litany or a myriad of other possible prayer forms, does not matter so much as the inward experiencing.

Stress in workers' meetings, where they share ideas with each other, should not be upon *things;* when one worker exhibits notebooks, murals, posters, or other products from his group, others may go back to attempt to copy the end products with insufficient attention to the steps by which a group of young persons is led to the inward awareness or conviction that is illustrated through the products. Given a similar conviction, one group may express in one way, another in a totally different way. Like twig made lifeless when separated from vine, an activity or method is lifeless unless it serves some *need* in young persons' experiencing.

The question is not what the young people did in this unit, but *what the unit did to the young people.*

VII

YOUTH LEARNING THROUGH DIRECT EXPERIENCES

And be not conformed to this world: but be ye transformed by the renewing of your mind, that ye may prove what is that good, and acceptable, and perfect, will of God.   ROMANS 12:2

Young persons are busy learning every minute of their lives. Cut through a cross section of almost any learning experience, and immediately evident will be the operation of the person's own purpose. He has some reason, perhaps half-conscious, for wanting to find answer to this or that question; for overcoming this or that difficulty. He reaches for help. Finding, he examines and decides to accept or reject the help. If he accepts, he weaves into his ongoing system of thinking or acting.

Concern here is for church-guided learnings, in the direction of Christian living in the fullest sense: not alone knowledge about the Christian way, but full-hearted response and follow-through, until Christian motives reach out even into unconscious reactions. Goals for Christian teaching in the Sunday school, youth meetings, and the like are vaster than that young persons get their minds furnished with Biblical facts or have a mass of information about the church through the ages. Knowledge is to the good, and let it not be discounted. But the goal is a matter of the young person's full-orbed commitment. The *motive* for Christ-centered living must go back of the knowledge; *conviction* must suffuse the concepts; *confidence* for action must propel the ideals. The church attempts to "set the stage" for this full learning.

The worker with young people, then, serving them in the Sunday church school class or department, or meeting with them in evening fellowships or special activities, is concerned to find and use the fullest, most direct, and most productive methods for helping these young

90

persons learn for living. Experience and common sense suggest that when the learner is merely *listening* to words someone says, he may be virtually inactive; he may respond but tentatively; he may be but little changed in his attitudes or even ideas for having listened. On a higher level of efficacy as a method of learning (because it involves the learner more fully himself) is *observation* on his part —seeing, either through pictures or going to see for himself. Yet even here the learner may remain merely spectator, giving but little of himself and gaining but little.

On a much higher level of effectiveness, because the learner is involved more deeply, is learning through *vicarious experience*. The learner moves over from the role of spectator to feeling-with a person or situation. On the highest level, because potentially involving the learner more fully, is firsthand, *direct experiencing*. Let us turn to examine possibilities along these lines for "regular" church work with young people in such meeting times as the Sunday school class, evening meeting, and the like.

Direct, Firsthand Experience

How can a young person learn the meaning of "community service?" Through finding a need, planning with his fellows what should be done, and following-through in positive action. How can a learner discover what "worship" means? Through worshiping in spirit and in truth. *After* experiencing, discussion may clarify understanding and help organize impressions. How can a young person "come alive" as to what world friendship involves? Through making world friends, and giving.

"Direct" experiences do not always involve physical activity, trips, and the like. Rather, the question is what takes place *within* the young person. A group may visit a scene. But unless they feel the grip of the needs thus witnessed, and decide, and do, perhaps they have merely observed. They have been exposed; the problem did not "take."

One worker at a training school heard about "learning through doing." To her, the word "doing" suggested paper work. She set her intermediates to cutting Palestinian figures as "activity." A visitor asked a boy at one juncture, "Why are you cutting that out?" "Because she said to!" he spat out like an explosion. What was he learning? Outwardly, it might appear that he was co-operating with the teacher's wish. But deep inside, might he not have been learning *directly* to feel resentment at teacher or at an activity for which the purpose was not clear to him, or which he had had no share deciding upon. (And might the teacher have been learning *directly* to foist her will upon young persons, without giving them sufficient opportunity for thinking of needs, planning, and deciding?) One learns his own reactions.

These intermediates might have read a certain dramatic episode from Bible times, then pictured it in their minds as if in technicolor. They might have decided to act the scene out for a later parents' meeting. Suppose that as they worked they encountered some jealousies and rivalries for choice parts. Suppose they had paused to face these difficulties squarely as young Christians through talking them over and even praying that God's help be with them. Suppose that in the final time of sharing others, too, had become more deeply aware of the Christian message through their own sincerity shining through. Contrast the values of the fuller experience of "living it out" with merely illustrating through paper figures.

Are there some types of direct experience not beyond the range of possibility for an average Sunday school or evening group of intermediates, seniors, or older youth? Young persons become bored with activities they suspect the adult worker has "made up" to keep them out of mischief. But they respond wholeheartedly to the pull of real work that needs doing in a real world! Does a worker have difficulty getting his young people to discuss? Let them experience a need, feel its pull. They will talk because they will have a *reason*. Discussion will be, not a method, but the inevitable response of young persons because something has gripped them and they must prepare to do something about it. Church work with young people in the past has done too little exposing of them to the real problems of the real world, and has offered too little challenge to *do* or guidance in finding the places to take hold even now at their age as youth. Too often, the idea of making a difference is left for some vague tomorrow when they grow older. To be sure, many and vast are the problems about which young persons cannot make a difference now; but likewise, many and vast are the ones where they can. The following are but illustrative:

1. *Making of their own group fellowship in the church a "laboratory" for Christian living.* Is there a clique that makes some feel frozen out? Is there some young person who feels inferior and neglected? What is happening to the in-group if it practices rejection of others? What can be done by young people themselves, and not just by the adult worker, to help the isolates and fringers feel more at home? To welcome newcomers and assure them of a place in the fellowship?

A church fellowship becomes a laboratory for good thinking also. Where big issues are skimmed over lightly for lack of time, or lack of preparation on the part of the youth-planning committee or adult worker, or mental laziness—is not slovenly thinking being practiced (and therefore learned)? Where religious ideas are left in a vacuum apart from life, is not the habit of thus compartmentalizing being learned?

Young persons set themselves up organizations with officers they elect. The efficiency and consecration with which they fulfill their responsibilities can be learning-for-life. Habit patterns are forged in early years. The church of tomorrow needs a generation of doers, not just members who are satisfied to talk about the great ideas of the Christian religion but who are unwilling to follow through in positive action. Humility of spirit in group quest betokens growing maturity.

Group discussions furnish laboratory for learning. One discovers that when he relinquishes his pet idea for a better one someone else suggests, the whole group's benefit is a result. Pooling thoughts instead of fighting one another's points develops a greater fund of group wisdom.

2. *Visits with definite purpose and careful evaluation and follow-through.* Depending on the need and the units under way, young persons may visit under guidance, factories, museums, churches, synagogues, industries, farms, homes, and the like. When a trip is

93

contemplated, contacts would need to be made with local leaders, ascertaining their willingness to have a group visit, and inviting them to share in the evaluation. All courtesies should be shown. The whole experience is an extension of the Christian fellowship being achieved in the class or group, into wider relationships with others. A spirit of respect and appreciation should pervade, not of paternalistic looking-down on a situation of need.

When young persons go out on evangelistic teams for visiting unreached and inviting them to join the fellowship group and the Christian way, something happens in the hearts of the visitors themselves and not alone in the hearts of those visited. Only through doing such jobs do they gain confidence and overcome fears.

3. *Interviews* may be made, when information is needed such as interviews can supply. (With this as with any method, it should be used only as needed, when almost inevitable.) Sometimes, the young people go to the interviewee. Sometimes, they invite resource persons to come to their meetings in the church. Fairness to a visitor should prompt them to acquaint him ahead of time with their questions and needs. Merely asking "outside speakers" to talk to their group about just anything may prove for the young people a way of learning irresponsible listening! (Dictators prey upon such.)

4. *Creating* for themselves. The word "creative" has been much used and misused. Not every experience of young people can, or *should* be "creative" in the literal sense. When a young person expresses in his own way something he sincerely feels, that expression is "creative." He, being unlike anyone else in the world, is expressing something new, something all his own. He is creating.

Not all "creative" expression need be visible or audible or tangible. Mistakenly, the word is often associated with products in the arts, exhibits, and such. But persons can be "creative" in human relationships as well.

Everyone knows the keen enjoyment that goes with creating—whether it be a nicely-turned corner while driving, or a cake browned to a turn, or a conversation reaching that warm glowing agreement that is the essence of fellowship. One can remember childhood excursions into doing-for-self: maybe assisting father with a repair

94

job, or cooking a meal without help, or making a play-theater for those exciting back-yard dramas to which the neighbors would be invited. No doubt such things could have been done better by an adult, so far as the product goes. But in them was something of one's *self*. One had put forth energy and time and imagination and here was a result! Each achievement has its own lead-on to further trying.

No adult worker can start cold with a group saying, "Go to, now; this morning we shall create." No. Any true creating comes unawares as a by-product when young persons are warmed and thrilled and enkindled into new experiences until expression comes spontaneously and almost inevitably!

The role of the adult worker is to set the stage, then to encourage young persons to "try their wings." Some get as far as the threshold but lose courage.

The adult can also help young persons recognize different channels they may choose for their expression. Too much emphasis has been placed on having youth "get up and take part" meaning *speaking* parts. But the Creator did not endow all with eloquent speaking abilities. Not everyone will find his natural channel in that direction. Some work better with their hands. Some cannot write but can cook. Some cannot sing or paint but can make others around them feel happy. Who is to say that the one is the more "creative" than the other? A wider channel of possibilities should be offered in the church, with no emphasis or prestige whatever placed on speaking or office-holding for they may be minor in the long view and actually less creative!

That young people be encouraged to make expression in some way for themselves is important. Persons today are too prone to be passive spectators on sidelines, viewing games, listening to music, seeing television and movies. The world needs creators in literature, music, drama, art, and other forms of mass communications. The church can help awaken slumbering aspirations, touch off the spark. In the old days, the church was custodian of the arts. Now it is custodian of the potentialities wrapped up in young spirits for creative expression, that personalities may be liberated and the world be blessed.

Young people can work together in groups to create. A class or evening group may form a prayer litany . . . letting suggestions come from several as to what they feel they wish to talk with God about, letting a secretary note the ideas, and then possibly letting a committee put the whole into form with a chosen refrain that all will use as their prayer channel. Records may be group-made of findings through discussion and research: logbooks, diaries, exhibits, newspapers, mimeographed write-ups, and the like. "We-did-it" feelings are more productive as direct experience than merely "I-did-it." The former usher in learnings of group co-operation, teamwork, fair play, and weness.

Activities that require persons to move about and use physical energy should be used occasionally with intermediates. Church rooms for all age levels should allow for moving chairs about the room as needed; and equipment should include small tables, not the long unwieldy kind. Young persons have "muscle hunger." They cannot sit long at a stretch and maintain zest. Elbows nudge neighbors; feet curl around chair rungs; dynamic energy awaits the press of a button. Unless channeled in constructive, purposeful ways, it may find expression in socially disruptive and individually harmful behavior.

5. *Group discussion* reaches the level of direct experiencing only when the individuals feel urgently the need to talk over a problem that is real to them; when they enter in; when they grapple through to some solution or course of action. Otherwise, the only element of direct experiencing may be in the phrasing of arguments, or in learning to be content with talk or resolution-passing. Some occasions when discussion may prove a pathway to direct experience (and not a substitute for one more direct, such as visiting a situation or engaging in service action):

a. When there is a problem upon which a divergence of opinion is felt.

b. When there are misunderstandings among the members of the group itself, that need clearing up.

c. When group members have sufficient background of experience and information about a problem, but need now to sort and arrange their impressions into useful categories, and to formulate plans ahead.

d. When a matter is confused or not quite clear.

Learning the "etiquette" of discussion may in itself be a direct experience. The atmosphere should be frank and free. Everyone should feel he can speak his mind without fear or bias or hesitation. Members should learn to listen respectfully to one another's contributions, and not talk when another is talking. Self-consciousness disappears as young people learn to concentrate on the problem at hand rather than upon themselves or upon what others may be thinking of them.

Only through doing can they learn to express thoughts briefly and clearly, not to speak unless they have something to say that contributes to the subject and the group's needs at the time. The adult can help, particularly with intermediates and seniors, by asking thought-provoking questions (not the yes-no or obvious-answer kind that affront youth's intelligence); by maintaining poise and unhurried spirit yet keeping track of the time, so that some stopping-point may be reached with a sense of achievement in the time available; by keeping track of points made on blackboard or chart; by drawing in hesitant members (tactfully, never forcefully) and by encouraging the too-talkative to give others opportunity; and particularly by narrowing and sharpening the issue until it *can* be dealt with; then by leading the young people in making their *own* summary and tabulation of conclusions, and possibly expression in prayer.

Discussion in youth groups, whether Sunday school class or evening meeting, *must* be adult-guided—whether the adult is sitting in the group circle unobtrusively or up in front. In the name of "youth participation" (but often without the actual spirit or realization), many evening fellowships of intermediates or seniors have been left to flounder hopelessly in attempts to have discussions without sufficient adult help. A young person has not lived long enough, or seen deeply enough into the problem at hand to guide those his own age in reaching solutions. Net results when young people try to lead discussion are usually that: (1) the issue is left in midair; or (2) a deadlock of differing views perplexes, that youth themselves

97

without help cannot break. Far fuller and more meaningful (and therefore more satisfying to the youth themselves) "participation" takes place when a prepared adult guides, drawing in the shy members, and helping move the discussion along toward goals.

Worship, the most deep-reaching and direct experience of all, can have a place in discussion meetings. But let it be understood that worship is not just a vague diffusion of reverential feeling. The young people should know, consciously, the very moment they pause to seek clearer vision from God; to pray for keen minds to think straight; to ask for courage. Worship does not begin until hearts focus Godward. The worship experience is God-centered, whereas discussion or other learning experiences are centering for the time being (and rightly so) on the problem at hand, using the minds and abilities God has given. As a group faces some difficult decision, members may need God's help; then their pause for a moment of silence or prayer is sincere, not a mere routine or form. As one young person put it, "We give God an 'in' in our discussion, for our own human minds are not enough."

When persons strive unselfishly and intelligently to find solutions to problems, however small the problems may appear, they are having a significant *direct* experience of group teamwork. They are practicing principles of fellowship and brotherhood. The world needs persons skilled in group discussion with brotherly spirit. The more young people learn to "winnow wisdom" from one another, from their resource helps, and from Above, then go forth to carry out group plans to make situations around them more Christian, here is Christianity as a *direct experience!* The Word become flesh.

6. *Activities for sharing with and serving others.* Too often in youth classes and meetings in the church, the allotted time is up before the group finishes! There is no rounded-out, achieving feeling. Next Sunday will be a different lesson. And so, week after week, there is failure to reach workable conclusions. They *learn* (through what they experience thus directly) that in matters religious, one does not nail the nail down; one does not bother to come to grips or decide; one leaves matters conveniently suspended or in the teacher's pious-sounding words as he tries hurriedly to tack a moral on; one

lets the other fellow be the one to *do* something about the ideas of the Christian faith. No wonder Protestant young people are so hard put to it to *tell* other youth what their churches stand for, what their basic beliefs are, what their stands are on social issues. Protestant young people, in hurried minutes of Sunday school classes and in ill-prepared "part-reading" programs Sunday evenings, have not had *practice* (direct experience) of "coming all the way through" to convictions, and of putting their convictions into words. John Wesley's class meetings in early Methodism, the gatherings of Quakers, and small-group fellowships of other religious bodies gave churchmen *practice* in telling to one another what the Lord had done for them! Having practiced, they could then tell the world.

"Lack of time" is the oft-cited difficulty. *Why* lack of time? Young people (and their workers) can always find time to do that which they want most to do. In every church there is *some* time for work with youth. Is it spent wisely?

The basic need is deeper than need for more time. It is a need for opportunities when the young people can clinch their decisions, put their findings and thoughts into words, crystallize their beliefs growing out of each specific unit—in short, summarize *for themselves* so that they *know* where they stand. A further deepening takes place when in addition they do something to share with others: invite parents for a summary session or give a special program to the church congregation, for example.

A time budget may be made, with youth helping plan, at the outset of each new unit: roughly how much time on this question in the unit and how much on that. Time can be allowed for unhurried drawing together of findings. Better one great idea followed through until the young people *feel* its meaning, and *know* their convictions, than a dozen different subjects skimmed shallowly.

Summarizing, and putting thoughts and findings into words, can be done *only* by the young people—*never* an adult. If the youth have not gotten something by the close of a unit, it is too late.

Ways they may choose for telling others of their discoveries may include: preparation of exhibits, posters, murals, marionettes, use of stories, drama, radio news flashes, and the like. The emphasis is not on the medium chosen for the sharing, but on the motive. Do the young people have something building up in their own experience they want to share? In a senior unit on "Planning for Tomorrow's World," a United Nations conference table was staged; the panel was planned by the youth themselves outlining the international problems and the Christian imperatives. A group mimeographed findings from an alcohol unit and distributed them to church members after worship!

7. *Loving concern for others expressed in plans and projects to help answer human need* is the most vital and valuable form of direct experience for young persons eager to understand what it means to follow Him who said, "The Spirit of the Lord is upon me . . . to heal, set at liberty, etc." Jesus' own life focus was Godward and others-ward. The experiences of young persons in the church should not be focused inward ("What a wonderful youth organization we have!" "How much we enjoy our activities together!" "How clever we have become!"). Rather, their experiences should be focused ever outward and upward in humility and love. The way to keep this focus is to give service action high priority.

There is no way to love God without serving people. Young people cannot learn this truth until they live it. "Why call ye me Lord if ye do not the things . . .?" If a youth movement is to emerge in our day, it will be because young people have set forth to serve and to give in the expectant spirit of being "about their Father's business" in building the world better. They can take hold on seemingly small and ordinary jobs in their own communities, in confidence that God can piece together the pattern of a better world from millions of small things done in His name. Later, when their channels of influence widen and their abilities are developed and disciplined, they may help bring Christian viewpoints into wider reaches of relationships.

Each unit of printed curriculum for young people should be approached as a "slice of life"—a unit of *study-and-service,* not alone of study. Depending on the specific area or problem with which the unit deals, ideas for service action should grow naturally from the discussions and other activities, inculcating awareness or concern.
100

The "other half" of real learning has not taken place until follow-through is made in some way—not always in overt action, to be sure, but first in changed attitudes, deepened concern, and more times than not in active service for somebody or some group or in battling the evils in some situation.

Once young people feel the tug of "real work in a real world," where they believe God would have them serve, their response will be zestful and voluntary. A further important direct experiencing takes place as they pause, not rushing ahead impulsively into possibly unwise action, to seek guidance and plan carefully and prayerfully. Further learning and growth in teamwork takes place when they seek advice from community agencies, or band together across denominational or faith lines in their action projects. They learn what they *live*.

VIII

YOUTH LEARNING THROUGH VICARIOUS EXPERIENCES

And this I pray, that your love may abound yet more and more in knowledge and in all judgment; that ye may approve things that are excellent. PHILIPPIANS 1:9-10a

Vicarious Experience

We are examining kinds of *experiences* young persons are having while learning, in terms of the degree the learner himself is actively involved: puts himself into it, wants to find help, actively reaches, thinks through, relates. One does not "learn" first in an abstract way through words merely, then later attempt to "express" in "activity," or "apply." The learning is in and through and because of the doing. "The lesson," therefore, is not the mere verbalization in a Sunday school class with "activity" as something separate later or as an accessory or extra if time allows. "The lesson" is what John and Jeanie *do* and *think* and *feel* and *decide* morning, evening, any time; putting ideas into words may be the least significant part of the learning experience.

Focusing on how the church may lift its work with young people to higher levels than that of learner-listening, we have looked at *direct experiencing* as the level of highest efficacy because it involves the learner most fully. Next is the level of vicarious experience.

This involves much more than merely looking at something or listening, although it may utilize both. It means entering imaginatively into the thoughts and feelings of others—"living over" experiences with them to the extent of one's sympathetic spirit, one's empathy, one's appreciative awareness, one's ability to project one's self over into the shoes of others or into a different situation. To an extent all persons have such abilities; little children are rich in their capacities to "feel with." Perhaps, in a technological era, persons

102

succumb to pressures on every hand to become literalistic, mathematical. Imaginations become tethered to stern realities.

To suggest much fuller use of this level of learning with young people is *not* to imply turning from careful, realistic approaches to the world as it is. It *is* to imply nurturing within them the God-given capacity to dream and to reach out with warm human understanding toward others!

Vicarious experiences, because they involve emotions, "go deep." What young people *feel* stays with them, and probably influences their actions far more than workers realize. What they know with their minds gets related to actions only through their feelings. Sympathetic awareness or fellow-feeling needs to be deepened today among the peoples of the world, that it may melt barriers. A study of world friendship that helps young people become more sympathetically aware of friends near and far may deeply affect their feelings and thus supply the needed incentive for their giving of their funds and ultimately, perhaps, of their lives.

What are some aids that may be used in "regular" church work with young people, to bid for this vicarious experiencing?

1. *Meaningful use of carefully-selected stories.* All the world loves a story! The worker with young people can improve his skills in the fine art of storytelling, and can encourage young people themselves to do so. Children's workers make abundant use of stories; perhaps fuller use may be made with intermediates, seniors, and older youth. Too often, when used, they are not used wisely and well!

For example, in some churches, apparently the use of stories is thought of in connection with "devotionals"—yet, upon analysis, this devotional or worship period should instead be God-centered rather than instructional. The function of the story is to impart information and to bid for vicarious identification; when used as a part of a learning process when the thoughts thus gathered can be discussed and further evaluated, the story proves tremendously useful. But in average Sunday school "devotionals"—aside from a vague moralistic tone—the long and sometimes highly symbolic stories tend to focus minds upon a subject other than that which will be discussed later

103

in the lessons units, and to take up time needlessly both from the God-centered worship experience and from the lesson following.

In a class group or youth fellowship, in the ongoing unit, one or several little stories may be needed. Let the atmosphere be created, either by the setting around the group, or by the very spirit of the storyteller. At a campfire out-of-doors, it may be easier for a group to transport themselves in imagination to the campfires of Hebrew nomads as they moved from one watering place to another, and paused at nightfall for the oldest member of the tribe to recount the ever-thrilling story of Jehovah's dealings with His people . . . episodes of epic grandeur imparting a sense of security and infinite worth to the individual and to the group. Or perhaps the young people are having a unit on devastation wrought by war and pathways to peace and they have a refugee campfire, imagining how homeless peoples must feel; perhaps a sacrificial meal can be partaken around the fire, with offering for relief. In their meeting room in the evening, the lights may be shaded for a folk-story hour; or in candlelight, the biography of a giant of the Christian faith may walk into their very midst, thrilling them with the possibilities in human personality when the living God works through someone. Music or pictures used along with stories may help enhance the meanings.

Stories may also be used to startle. At the beginning of a unit opening up a raw problem in human relationships, a story may be launched right into—with no attempt to build atmosphere first. The impact of the facts will speak for themselves. Committees of young people, assisting the adult worker in planning for their units for Sunday school and evening meeting, may find and prepare such "openers." Excerpts from the best works of modern fiction and drama may help bring problems before the youth. The relating of recent incidents in community life may point up the stark need for doing something about the evils thus felt. With such situations, a leader may leave a story unfinished, challenging the group to decide what the ending should be.

2. *Moving drama.* The range of possibilities in drama is vast: chancel dramas or pantomimes to lead young people to a sense of reverence and perhaps a desire for commitment in worship; a drama

that follows faithfully in costume and scenery the original story so as to impart as true-to-life impressions as possible; a drama in modern dress that puts punch back of one central point; shadow dramas that aid in creating mood; brief one-scene episodes, radio dramas, or recordings that open up problems and provoke discussion; marionette and puppet shows that depict stories, entertain, or deal with problems; dramatic dances that nurture religious aspirations or express worship; living pictures that illustrate great ideas; dramatization of an oratorio or anthem to enhance meaning and deepen emotions; role-playing that encourages individuals to identify emotionally with other persons in order that they may be enabled to solve problems in tense relationships or in order that they may understand more fully and clearly how these other persons felt or feel; psycho-drama that gives opportunity for overt expression of rankling inner tensions; socio-drama that gives opportunity for depicting social situations and the give-and-take of many individuals involved; ceremonials at special times during the church year, or when the young people feel the need for such, or when they have experiences that demand special worship celebrations.

Intermediates, seniors, and older youth all thrill to opportunities for making up their own dramatic versions of story material or biographies that have gripped them. When kept simple and to-the-point, drama is an excellent way for young people to crystallize their ideas and put them into such form as can be shared with others.

When original plays are being prepared, adult workers need to guide the young people in organizing their plans, not attempting too much! There may be a tendency to distort the story, and here an opportunity for tactful counseling will appear; the group may be led to refer carefully to the Bible narrative or the source for their work. The discipline of faithfulness in portrayal is a valuable learning. Undue attention should not be devoted to scenery, settings, or wordings that might get in the way of the central focus always on the Big Idea or meaning they are seeking to get across.

Great dramas may be performed sincerely by young people, particularly by older youth. The very preparation of one of the vital religious dramas can be a deepening experience for young people, one they

105

will never forget. Always, with any use of drama, the emphasis is upon what is happening inside the young persons and also what may happen to audiences under the spell of the drama's message as revealed *through* them—rather than emphasis upon "putting on a performance."

Often some "direct" learnings occur as young persons decide together upon a story or message to dramatize, plan, and write the script, work out the play. Problems may arise; as they are faced carefully and prayerfully, the members grow. Drama proves an excellent vehicle for promoting co-operation in a group. Even as the individuals learn to "identify" themselves with the character they are portraying in a particular story, they learn also to identify imaginatively with members of their own group, thus growing in their understanding of one another and their abilities to work together as young Christians.

3. *Visual helps.* Later, under "observation" as a level of learning, attention will be given to procedures for using pictures, flat or projected. Not all observation moves beyond seeing and assimilating to that deeper awareness and self-forgetting in vicarious experience. One passes over a mysterious threshold from beholding to being, to feeling-with. One "loses himself" in the scene.

Sound movies, perhaps particularly those in color as being closer to "real life," bid more than other media for this entering in. In fact, one of the dangers regarding movies of any kind is that a person young or old can scarcely *keep from* losing himself in the story, and thus becoming powerfully influenced by it—for better or for worse. The more dramatic the story and the more sincere the action, the fuller will be the vicarious experience. Some Bible dramas have been produced in sound movies that prove unforgettable in their impact. Because the medium has such a high potential for influencing learning, any movies or other projected visual helps should be chosen with utmost care and with relation to the experiences and needs of the particular age level.

When used for the purpose of helping young persons vicariously experience some significant idea, preparation for visuals must needs be particularly careful. The worker must sense what the visual does.

How? Through the window of his own experience. He should preview, thinking of the group's need, possible confusions the showing might engender, ways of preparing the members for the seeing and ways of following up afterward.

4. *Service action* may bring to the learner some direct experiences and some vicarious experiences at the same time. A visit is made to a situation of need; response is genuine, and some project of action is planned. Probably a component part of the response, and the motive for helping, comes from sympathetic awareness, which can be close to Christian love.

There are many ways young persons can serve and give to needs far away. Denominations have missions enterprises, and some have special youth funds. Stories of what is being accomplished in those fields, or of the heroism and consecration of missionaries, or of the response of young persons like themselves in other lands can move upon the hearts of young people and establish that intangible yet powerful bond of fellow-feeling and love across oceans. Units on prayer may make use of prayers of young Christians in other lands, that the world may be truly "at one" in prayer.

To an extent, younger youth who are not yet old enough to hold office in wide-area youth organizations, can "identify" with the thrilling accomplishments of their older brothers and sisters and their youth fellowship of which organization they in their own church are a part. There is a similar "weness," and hence security in a worth-imparting relationship built around the self, in school spirit, or even in patriotism. When representatives of their youth organization do volunteer service in work camps, short-term missions projects and the like, the younger youth through vicarious identification can in a sense participate with them. Such identification is needed for intercessory prayer to be full-meant.

As young people are guided in Christian stewardship, they can be helped to make vicarious identification with the persons serving "in their stead" in the local community and wider world. One's money placed reverently in the offering plate as an act of worship is one's "coined energy" being sent to far corners of the earth.

5. *Games* prove another interesting medium for deepening appre-

ciations. A group of intermediates tried to learn a certain Chinese game and found it intricate. Their respect for Chinese boys and girls who could play such a game skillfully grew by leaps and bounds. The adult workers felt that here a "fellow-feeling" had been called forth that would probably never have come through discussion alone. As young people over America (and indeed in various parts of the world) learn to play and sing the folk songs and rhythmic games of the nations, surely this sharing of fun is a foundation for uniting the peoples!

6. *Verse speaking, group reading.* Voices, tested according to quality (not pitch) and grouped for "light," "dark," "medium" tones, may read together until they achieve smoothness, rhythm, and ability to express meanings. Poetry, original descriptive verse (such as may be written by the young people themselves), and Bible passages may be rendered with beauty, feeling, and worship value. Group reading is a somewhat new technique for church workers, although long used by folk of other lands and by persons of many racial and cultural groups. Imagine a group of young people seated in a circle around a campfire with Bibles open to a chosen passage. The entire group reads the narrative part, and solo voices take the conversational parts. A feeling of reality pervades.

There are many other media for helping young persons achieve vital and valid vicarious experience. Practically any of the methods a worker can name could, at one time or another, be lifted to this level. The above appear to be those methods that lend themselves most readily and immediately to the achievement by the learner of sympathetic awareness, appreciation, "entering in."

Never should this level be taken as a *substitute* for direct experience! Young people need to have their hearts warmed . . . but they need guidance also in moving them forward to the next step: that of following through their Christian concern into action.

IX

YOUTH LEARNING THROUGH
OBSERVATION

*In the visions of God brought he me into the land of Israel, and
set me upon a very high mountain. . . .*   EZEKIEL 40:2

Observation

We have been examining "levels" of learning, in terms of the extent
of the learner's own full-orbed purpose and participation. In the
preceding chapters, we saw *direct* firsthand experience on the part
of the learner as most efficacious, with *vicarious* experience second.

Moving downward in ratio of value in the learning experience is
the learner's engaging in *observation*.

This is a picture-minded age. More and more magazines use more
and more space for illustrations. Public schools and now churches are
making vast strides in visualizing their curricula.

Looking at the *real thing* is, to be sure, more effective as a learning experience, than seeing pictures of it. The use of pictures,
whether flat or projected, cannot be thought of as substituting for
trips, interviews, or other more direct contacts. Often, the seeing of
a need for one's self will awaken sympathies and motivate plans for
action—thus ushering in vicarious experiences of fellow-feeling and
direct experiences of serving and giving.

Visual resources are becoming available to an increasing extent
for church use. The list of helps is varied and flexible, but selections
should be made with utmost care. The adult worker and if possible a
committee of young people should preview before showing to the
group, to be sure that the resource will fit in with the group's ongoing
experience in its present unit process, or answer the group's need
at a particular stage.

The motive for using such a resource is not to allow the adult

109

worker to escape needed preparation for teaching. Nor is a motive that of merely entertaining the young people. Occasionally inquiries are made by ministers as to what films they can get to "attract" more young persons to their church groups. The truth is that inasmuch as movies are such a common experience, youth are rarely "attracted," particularly if the showings are not related to a fuller, more vital discussion in which those who come feel they are *getting somewhere*. A sense of achievement does help persons want to continue to come. There is little challenge in coming just to be attracted, or entertained.

Shall a movie be used or slides or filmstrips? Usually a movie depicting different scenes and actions, particularly if it has a sound track, will create more of a sense of reality than still pictures, although kodaslides and filmstrips, especially when in color, make deep impressions. An advantage in slides and filmstrips is that they may be held on the screen while discussion takes place. But if the purpose in the showing is to deepen appreciations, stopping for discussion would be unwise; the group would need more the over-all emotional impression.

Teachers' and counselors' notes for the youth curriculum units suggest visual and auditory materials along with printed ones; and often carry hints as to possible stages in the unit process where a showing would prove fitting. Particular attention should be paid to the suggestions for preparing members of the group for the showing, and following through by relating to the unit.

Extreme care should be exercised in choosing what to use. Only those visual and auditory media should be used that are theologically sound, grounded in Biblical scholarship, and imparting impressions in line with healthy personality growth. That which enters through the eyegate is imprinted indelibly upon sensitive young minds. Pictures that might impart an idea of God or Jesus that will have to be unlearned with difficulty later should be avoided at all odds, no matter how pious the purpose or how persuasive the advertising. Only the best in religious art, drama, filming, or radio work should be allowed.

Among nonprojected visual helps may be listed such types as:

110

1. Flat pictures, cartoons, photographs, post cards, text and reference book illustrations;
2. Maps, diagrams, charts, graphs, time lines;
3. Models, collections, curios, globes, specimens, aquaria, apparatuses, costumes;
4. Articles created by young people themselves such as posters, murals, friezes, scrapbooks, newspapers, collections, maps, diagrams, exhibits, charts, time lines.

Some teachers mistakenly wait until they can show a projected picture of some length, when all the while flat pictures or other aids would have been readily available. There is an advantage in having inexpensive, ready-to-use helps that the young people can handle at close range. Denominational periodicals and picture sets may be drawn upon as a primary source. Individuals in a church may donate offerings for purchasing sets of flat pictures to form a church school art library. As with projected pictures, preparation of the group for the use of the pictures will insure a fuller response and clearer understanding.

In addition to the familiar types of projected aids (movies, filmstrips, slides) there are stereoscope and stereographs, and opaque projection. In some church activities, television is now being used.

Through all such media run dynamic potentialities. Peoples of other nations and times can walk into a class or meeting. Entrancingly, they can show their customs and traditions, their achievements and problems in realistic and lifelike situations. They can enthrall one with drama, and turn drab and everyday happenings into something glorious or tragic as the case may be. Social attitudes may be created, problems laid with inescapable challenge upon the soul. Appeal is not only to the mind but to the emotions as well, whence the springs of actions come.

Three safeguards should be thrown around the use of any projected media:

1. That the showing of pictures never be considered a substitute for direct experiences on the part of the young persons themselves.

The picture may introduce, the direct experience come later, as has been pointed out above. Let no worker or youth committee schedule a "showing" as substitute for their own hard-bitten thought and "coming to grips" in their classes and meetings. The teacher who, having booked fifty-two films and counted his lesson-preparation problems solved for the year, was suffering from a delusion as to what teaching means (or else avoiding the task of making proper preparation). Actually, *more* preparation is needed, in terms of how prepare the group for a film and how to follow up afterward.

2. That the seeing of pictures, especially of projected media, not be regarded by the young persons themselves as entertainment but rather as a means of achieving solutions to their problems, or as a means of helping them prepare to worship God. Church showings should promote, rather than limit, youth's active participation. There is, however, an "entertainment complex" generally as persons carry over from movies and television where they are passive spectators. This will have to be overcome when projected aids are used for different purposes. Young persons themselves (and not alone their leaders) should have *purpose* in using visuals, just as they need purpose in using printed helps. Any picture or other aid takes its place—perhaps in some situations quite a minor place—in the larger learning experience.

3. Adequate preparation should be made, so that the group knows what to look for and why. They need, too, to be emotionally prepared—particularly when the film is to be one leading to worship.

4. Needless to say, when projected media are being used, the adult and youth committees should see to it that all equipment is in perfect order; that there is an extra bulb; that the film is in the projector and focused ready for use before the first person comes; and that where recordings are to be used as with filmstrips, the persons running both machines rehearse together. Above all, the picture must be previewed carefully. If it contains any potentially harmful suggestions, let it be returned without showing, no matter how much has been paid for its rent!

Denominational and interdenominational sources publish catalogues and film reviews. There is an abundance of material from

112

which to choose. Bookings should be made far enough ahead to allow sufficient time for shipment before the desired date. Return should be prompt and the materials in perfect condition.

In newer church buildings outlets are being included for audio-visual equipment—*not just in one large room* for mass showing as in the old days, but rather in each classroom so that teachers can utilize these helps at appropriate stages in a group's experience.

What is the place of the adult worker with youth when using such media? What opportunity for youth participation?

The place of the teacher or counselor is the same as when any other tool is used. Subsequent suggestions will show how youth themselves can set up purposes in their units, and help plan activities of learning, on these various levels of efficacy according to the possibilities open before them. When young people and their leaders plan to use visual media, such purposes as the following may be in their minds:

1. To stimulate the interest of the members, or to awaken concern about a problem, or to help them want to discover more information.

2. To offer additional helpful information when young people need it as they work on a problem.

3. To clinch some truth they have first worked through for themselves.

4. To suggest some possible avenues for further action on their part.

Thus, the use of visual or other media neither precludes the adult's preparation nor the young person's active participation. In fact, *more* of both should be expected. The use of such media offers delicate problems, requiring *all the more careful preparation on the part of the adult leader*.

The time may come when lesson materials from denominational houses will use integrally prepared projected and printed materials. For some units, instead of the visuals supplementing the print, the situation may be reversed.

Television may prove revolutionary in all church work. The home may again become the focal center. Neighborhood gatherings in homes for television may generate more fellowship among people over denominational and faith lines. Children, youth, grownups and older adults may find new fellowship across age-group lines. The vital question is the nature of the programs offered. Church leaders of talent are urged to study the techniques of script-writing and production, and methods for using wisely such a powerful means of communication.

Imagination suggests high possibilities in home-education programs, with the Sunday work in the church building becoming increasingly supplementary. However, there will surely continue to be urgent need for young persons to have special fellowship experiences with others of their own age and interests, and guidance as they develop their own pulsing powers through active and purposeful participation.

X

YOUTH LEARNING THROUGH LISTENING

And he said unto me, Son of man, stand upon thy feet, and I will speak unto thee. And the spirit entered into me when he spake unto me, and set me upon my feet, that I heard him that spake unto me.　　　　　Ezekiel 2:1, 2

Listening

At the lowest level of learning, because it requires less of active participation on the part of the learner himself, is the experience of listening. Listening involves the young person in only a limited amount of activity. Only a part of his whole self participates.

To be sure, there are levels of listening—rare times when a person reaches for meanings wanted badly, or times when in story or drama there is that mysterious "entering in" that betokens vicarious identification. But for the most part, there is minimum response to words. Therefore, the young person learns but in a limited way, or he learns perchance in a distorted way. For the listener there is always a convenient escape: he can close his ears and mind or think about other things while apparently fixing his attention upon a speaker. Ears may serve as convenient parentheses for a blank.

Studies in communication in recent years are revealing in a startling way the weakness of mere words as a means of getting meanings across from person to person. Even where words are used rapidly and where fairly accurate meanings are apprehended, the listener may "learn" far more from the spirit the speaker radiates than from what he says. "What you *are* speaks so loudly I cannot hear what you say."

However, there are times (not so many, perhaps, as the teacher might like to think) when listening is the *only* avenue of response open to the young people: (1) when neither adult nor young people can go to see directly for themselves; (2) when they cannot have vicarious or otherwise direct experiences; (3) when they cannot find pictures or other visual helps.

All these other levels of learning make use of words. Words in turn have enhanced meaning when they accompany experiences of observation or vicarious or direct experience.

Some adult workers unwittingly tend to confuse teaching with talking. Words may not convey to the learner what the worker intends. The tone of voice may impart a meaning quite different from that of the words spoken, or may enhance that meaning manyfold. Music speaks a language universal. Pictures "tell." The former hierarchy of the words is fast toppling. The trend toward letting pictures convey quick meanings that "he who runs may read" accustoms young people to depending less upon words than was the case with generations past. What is more, the same word may convey widely-variant meanings to different persons in the same group. The word "music" may bring a surge of delight to one whose passionate hobby is classical records; it may call to mind blatant noisy jukeboxes to another. The "Our Father" concept may be colored by unhappy home experiences. Study into semantics and related problems of communication in recent years suggests the jeopardy to meanings risked when one moves from the immediate and concrete, through symbols and words "up the ladder of abstraction." The more generalized a term, the more vague its meaning, particularly to young persons.

If a worker's mainline concern as he prepares is for his own security, he will probably fall back on words. They are probably easiest for him to use. But if extent of actual teaching be measured by extent of learning (young persons learning through purposeful doing), then words may be less effective than direct or vicarious experiences prompted through use of pictures or trips. For the worker to prepare so that learnings may take place on these higher levels involves beginning farther ahead; brooks less bluffing; requires more complete plans for steps in a process of teaching-learning. But his efforts will be rewarded in fuller, richer learnings on the part of the young people themselves.

116

What are some situations in which groups will be dealing primarily on the level of listening? That is, when other methods are not needed?

1. *Questions.* The phrasing of a question by the worker should be carefully planned and geared to the age range of that particular group. Seniors and older youth can respond more readily and fully to questions than can intermediates. They have lived more meaning into words, they have broader ranges of experience, they have more ideas. Workers will learn to sharpen their questions to an edge, rather than leaving vague generalizations trembling in mid-air ("What is brotherhood?"). A question that implies a yes-no answer, or one that carries an obvious answer is an insult to young minds. Pious-sounding phrases in questions leave young persons unimpressed and possibly anaesthetize.

Good teaching is taking place, someone has suggested, when the young people themselves are asking the questions! The teacher has awakened them to sense some needs; their minds are stirring. They are seeking.

With younger youth, a story may be used first to furnish background, and questions for discussion may relate specifically to it—thus giving a place to take hold.

2. *Reading.* Reading may take place silently or aloud, individually or in groups. As will be shown in the following chapters, young people with their leader in the unit process may work in small groups to secure information to bring to the total group; they may read what is in the printed helps from their denominational headquarters, and explore other resources. This procedure of working in small groups at times is simple enough to lend itself for small-church use.

If reading aloud, young people will understand the need for keeping voices low in consideration of other groups working around in the same room. (This evidence of thoughtfulness is in itself a *direct* learning, regarding ways of getting along with others.)

The old practice of "reading verses around," or "reading parts" in Sunday school classes and youth meetings is worse than useless. It stultifies thinking and encourages lack of previous preparation. Particularly does it cripple youth's potential happy experiences with the

117

Bible. There are myriads of meaningful ways to read Bible sections individually and in groups. Occasionally, all the members may read together to catch the full sweep and majesty of the rhythms. Occasionally, each may read silently to himself to think through meanings, later to discuss with others. Whenever the Bible is to be used, let there be a spirit of anticipation built up—"Listen, the Bible is about to speak!"

3. *Use of radio, television, and other current news sources.* Young people may report on information gained through radio or television or otherwise. On rare occasions, portable sets may be brought for listening to certain broadcasts, with discussion afterward. Indiscriminate use of radio or television in the homes should be discouraged. Evaluation may be made of programs from time to time.

4. *Use of speakers and resource persons.* Too often in the past the teacher in the Sunday school hour has regarded himself as "speaker." Too often, too, young people in planning for evening meetings have turned to "speakers" as a way, perhaps, to avoid making necessary preparation for their own participation. There come times when learning takes place to the extent that a speaker does *not* talk! The leader who uses words when his young people at that moment might have had direct or vicarious experiences, closes a door. For him to tell them answers may be robbing them of the incentive and lasting value of finding out for themselves, possibly robbing them of a luminous moment of deeper awareness beyond words.

Young people in meetings they plan can rob one another of meaning by the old routine of "program parts." To be sure, printed materials may be used richly for guidance, but unless the young persons first master the ideas for themselves and then share them in a sincere and personal way, the chances are that they will not "come alive" for the others in the group. Likewise, there is a place at times for a resource speaker. But let him be brought in only when a group has exhausted its own ideas on the problem, and let him be apprised of questions they have raised, so that his suggestions may fit into their ongoing process of working on the problem. The group should continue to feel its own responsibility to grapple with the problem for itself.

118

What about the words adults use with youth? Studies have been made of vocabularies appropriate for various age levels. The denominational curricula follow closely the best findings. The need of young people is not so much for three-letter words (they often know long technical ones stumping their teachers), but rather for maximum of concreteness and of relation to immediate known experiences of their lives.

A word with rich meaning to an adult—a word spelled, perhaps with three letters—may fall on youth ears with all-but-meaningless sound. Why? Because it is an abstract concept, a generalization. And young persons have not yet lived long enough to fill these empty vessels with meaning. Words calling forth visual images are best of all. The Bible abounds in them.

Particularly are young persons on guard against pious phrases, clichés, glib platitudes. To be sure, some who wish to please the teachers may mouth such words themselves. But let them not be trained to practice hypocrisy.

This is not to rule out the use of "reverent" words, particularly in prayers. Young people sense when feeling is genuine behind a word. Sincere expressions count, whether meaning is fully clear or not. Some feel that "Thou" and "Thee" convey more reverence when addressing the Deity, than the commoner pronouns. Others say that they can put the same feeling into "You." Let any expression be used naturally and meaningfully and from the heart.

At no time should meanings be left "up in the air." If unfamiliar words are used with young people, let time be taken for them to work out definitions to the satisfaction of all. Biblical locations and proper names should be pronounced correctly the first time used and ever thereafter (else, wrong pronunciations or slovenly treatment is learned). Most Bibles have a dictionary of pronunciation. Or surely one can be borrowed from the pastor. To slide over names and meanings is to treat both the Bible and the young people with disrespect.

Young persons learn not alone from what they hear but by their *responses*. Their ears may hear one set of works; they may respond to the atmosphere of hurriedness and uncertainty the teacher exudes. Quietness and seeming receptivity are deceptive. They may be think-

119

ing about Friday night's party. Apparent assent may be deceptive also. Even if convinced intellectually, the young people may not yet have caused much change in their attitudes.

Some workers talk so fast and say so much that they leave few chinks of time in which the young people can assimilate, taste, mull over, interpret. "She talks so much we can't think." An adult trying to lead discussion throws out a question or two. Silence for the space of a split second. (Why do lapses of time seem longer to the teacher?) When no one speaks up, the teacher rephrases, this time adding more sentences and generally muddying the waters. By the time she finishes, the youth are lost. Noting their confusion, she quickly throws an answer into the gap, perhaps with a "don't you think?" to maintain a semblance of give-and-take. The strain over, the young people make assent with a sigh of relief. Workers who expect young people to think and to participate in discussion must give them time, as one said, to "arrange" their thoughts.

Young people may show politeness to the adult worker while inwardly dissenting. Or they may be too lazy to raise questions. Or the time may be too short. Or the subject may be far away from their concerns. Or they may draw a conclusion vastly different from that for which the teacher was bidding, and say nothing about it—while the teacher goes his merry way considering one more lesson "taught."

For a moment a word may hang in the air. Young ears may hear. But until young minds and hearts have taken the meaning and grappled with it, examined it, agreed or disagreed, and related it to their needs and deeds—have they *heard*. "Be ye doers . . ."

XI

YOUTH LEARNING THROUGH WORSHIP

*Now the God of hope fill you with all joy and peace in be-
lieving, that ye may abound in hope, through the power of the
Holy Ghost.* ROMANS 15:13

The church has a resource beyond that of any other agency: the
opportunity of helping young persons come into the presence of the
Great Counselor and put their hand in His to be led further along
the highroad of learning and living.

Worship itself can be an experience of *learning*. At first glance,
such a statement may appear sacrilegious. Yet worship *can* be an
"activity of learning." It can open the eyes. It can touch the heart
with new compassion for others in need. It can bring "conviction of
sin." It can usher in those "changes" that signify that learning has
taken place. Through worship, a plus element enters into the
process, over and above the helps supplied by the adult workers, the
printed resources, and the other tools.

To recognize God's part in the teaching-learning process should
be the worker's first step. Young people themselves can realize this
truth. How natural it should be for a group to pause a moment at
any point in their "journey" through a unit of study, to seek direction, or clearer sight, or needed courage—or perhaps out of exulta-
tion in new discoveries to thank God for minds to think His thoughts
after Him!

The more naturally and freely and confidently young persons
learn to worship God amidst their work and play together, the more
likely they will be to carry that spirit into their everyday living.
Their devotional lives will be strengthened, almost without their
consciously knowing it.

Unfortunately, there exists in the minds of many (young people

123

themselves as well as their adult helpers) a concept of worship as being somehow separate from classes or other activities of learning. They gather for Sunday church school. A period is set aside for "devotions." After the program, a leader announces, "Now you may go to your classes." It is as if someone said, "Worship is now over. The rest of the time we move into a different kind of experience."

To overcome this compartmentalization of worship from other aspects of youth work in the church, and its probable compartmentalization in their daily lives, young people and their workers should give careful and prayerful thought to ways of lifting all kinds of experiences to the worship level.

Sometimes in a class or evening meeting, the young people will wish to express their thoughts spontaneously in worship. It may be through a prayer or a litany, or even a song. When some original youth-expressed contribution is thus made, the hearts of all are touched for there is a ring of reality.

A moment of quiet before a class or meeting may enable group and leader to have a sense of Presence throughout the period. There will be an inner calmness that should enable them to think more clearly and to decide more truly, as in His sight.

Amidst discussion or other activities, the need may be felt for a pause for power, or for clarification. The group may have grown weary. The members may be tempted to give up on the problem. They may have become tense in a heated argument. They may have lost sight of the vision with which they started. Moments of silence first, and then perhaps a whispered prayer or fellowship of prayers . . . and then a new start, but with new clearness as of a summer sky cleared by showers.

Beginning a new unit and facing its adventurous pull, a group may seek God's guidance for their study. Should they not feel that they are working, not merely with one another and their teacher, but with an unseen Companion? Would not such a consciousness lend zest to their research, point to their discussions, and purpose to their decisions? Who knows but that such a spirit in a group might not in turn influence attendance and enrollment?

Closing a unit, and looking back over their findings, young people may wish to pray a spontaneous prayer of thankfulness for minds to think, for fellowship with one another, and for the very chance to "do something about" significant problems for the sake of the Kingdom.

When making a hard decision, coming to grips with the Christian imperative, young people will realize that changes must be made in their thinking, their attitudes, their actions. They may seek to know God's will more fully. Daily they should seek a fuller understanding of the way Jesus lived and taught. They may pray for strength of will to carry all the way through the decisions they have made, even as Jesus did with His decisions. They may pray that they, like Him, may give their *daily lives*.

The adult worker may hesitate, saying, "But I would be afraid I wouldn't know just how to handle such moments." One says, "The expression 'spontaneous worship' frightens me." If the springs of his own devotional life are deep, a teacher need not fear. He will be spiritually sensitized. He will know what to do . . . and what not to do. Likewise his young people will be sensitive.

Less Clutter and More Depth

Programs of youth fellowship activities in many churches are too cluttered for much real worship to take place often. In feverish effort to get across materials, or put programs over, or have lessons taught, adult workers may fail to open the way for young people to have those experiences of learning which, after all, are deepest and most abiding.

Youth these days live by clocks and datebooks. Whirl is king. In fact, they become feverishly caught up in motion: school, extra-curricular activities, social plans, clubs, dates. By and by they fear to have a half-hour of unregimented time on their hands, a moment to "stand and stare, to lie in the sunlight," to look quietly up into the starry heavens, to go to the top of a hill alone some lazy afternoon and dream.[1]

Schedules can be planned for church activities (with young people sharing in the planning, for many recognize this need) to streamline and cut down on nonessentials, and to give top-priority time to those things which are highest. Leaders with serenity are needed, too.

Picture a meeting room, carefully prepared and cleaned . . . a bowl of fresh flowers on the table . . . perhaps a screen or drape hiding any extraneous furnishing such as blackboard . . . materials put away in cupboards, not left lying around . . . at the center, placed so as to catch the eye of all who enter, one lovely picture—the kind of picture at which one can look and look and still see more . . . quiet music, playing for several minutes—long enough to weave a pool of reverent contemplation. Then, with such preparation of spirit, some moments for unhurried prayer. In terms of schedule, only a few minutes may have been consumed. Yet the experience of fellowship with God in worship may have been more real than with a program full of many items consuming long periods and involving much speaking.

Young persons need time to think, "for the thoughts of youth are long, long thoughts." The world has need of those thoughts! Yet when, in their crowded days, will they have time to think if the church not provide such time? Speedier becomes their tempo the older they grow. Junior high age boys and girls rush from school to music to club to play to something else. Their days are fraught with feverish hurry and their nights with nervous anxiety.

What a challenge to their church! Young persons of this generation need provision for quiet, unrushed moments in still, beautiful places where—with simple helps and not so much speaking—they may sink their thoughts deep into the eternal realities and find anchorage for their souls. "In quietness and confidence" shall be their strength. The mainline ministry of the church is to help them form beliefs and find communion with God as Father. They can then go forth with poise and a sense of mission, nerved of God to help work out His purposes in a needy world.

Less Hurry, and More Awareness

In a fairly small church, a group of intermediates was beginning a unit of study. The key thought of the unit, "My Father's Work and

124

Mine," was the dependability of God's universe. But those boys and girls, the leader knew, were not very clear about their ideas of God.

Their need was not for argument. Rather, it was for quiet thinking and feeling—in order that something of the harmony of the universe might seep into their souls and help them *know*. The teacher borrowed from the Primary Department a print of Taylor's "When I Survey Thy Heavens." Placing it where all could see (on their eye level), she did not try to "teach a lesson" (that is, in words) that morning. Together, they took time to look. (The message of great pictures cannot be apprehended at a glance . . . or of great music . . . or of great literature . . . or of Bible truths.)

Something about that picture helps one stand in imagination beside the lone shepherd as he looks up "in perfect stillness at the stars" (as one girl wrote in a poem she made about it). One said that as she looked, the sky seemed to grow darker and the stars brighter. No formal worship "service" was needed in that group that morning. Rather, just the chance to be aware. In moments like this, there is a sensing of Truth deeper than spoken word or phrase can bring. It falls upon the spirit as dew from heaven, bringing not alone knowledge, but feeling as well. Ever after, they can affirm, in the words Tennyson used for what must have been similar experiences, "I have felt."

Young spirits cannot be hurried in their becoming aware. Time must be taken. The adult who sits by the side of young persons must help them calm their anxious tensions and habit patterns, and with them "be still and know." Dare the teacher try it? Will not the intermediates giggle? Will not the seniors whisper? Will not the older youth condemn? No! For young persons are deeply responsive to that which is real. They are spiritually hungry. They will feel the contagion of sincere reverence.

A photographer had made some exquisite colored slides of nature scenes. He expressed misgivings when asked to show them at a summer camp of boys and girls. "Young people are so noisy," he remonstrated. But after the showing he came away humbled before their genuine response as evidenced in that "holy hush" that betokens a group entering deeper levels of awareness, and as evidenced by their scarcely-breathed "oh's" and "ah's."

An older youth group spent an evening hearing a florist describe the intricate processes by which he grew long-stemmed roses, orchids, and gardenias. The meeting had not been planned as a worship "service," and no formalities ensued. Yet the spirit of reverence had been present in the meeting. No amount of dissecting discussion could have done for the group what this deepening experience of appreciation did that night.

Workers may be concerned about the associations young persons carry with them from experiences they have had in the church. If a hymn, a verse of Scripture, or a principle of living has been treated casually in routine fashion, the chances are that they will so regard it next time . . . and the next . . . and on through life. But if it has opened for the young people a new window of thought or feeling, that association likewise will come back on wings of memory throughout life.

Not always can beauty and richness be brought into the classroom or meeting room. Sometimes the group itself needs to venture out into nature's cathedral, there to commune as silently and as long as desired. People these days probably tend to talk too much; fill the hours with radio or television sounds; spend too much time in man-made places with man-made gadgets. Some do thus to escape coming face to face with their souls.

Less Preoccupation with Programs, More Launching Forth Into Service

A visitor entered a Quaker meeting late; he whispered to his neighbor asking when the service was to begin. "The service begins when the meeting ends," he was quietly told.

A group of young persons may form habits of getting a pseudo-achievement through having a program *about* a problem instead of faring forth to see what could be done. The meaning of "worship" is misunderstood when it is regarded as an experience of contemplation only, in some retreat spot in soft light away from the busy marts of men. One draws apart to seek guidance and clarity of

126

perspective and inner quietness of spirit; but thus prepared, one moves bravely out into difficult situations to bring healing love and understanding. In the words of St. Francis, one prays that one might become an "instrument of Thy peace," sowing love where there has been hatred before. The more wholeheartedly one serves, the more urgent becomes his spiritual need for further strength and power and so he is driven to earnest worship; in turn, a new commissioning comes upon him as he worships so that he returns to serve with new mission. And so the spiral of spiritual growth moves ever upward and ever outward until through Christian love barriers are melted and brotherhood translated into realities in a humble, practical, down-to-earth sense.

A young man told how for years he had sought an experience of God such as others appeared able to describe; but somehow he felt he was always falling short of the awareness of presence he believed might be possible. One day, in a crowded intersection there was an accident. Utterly forgetting self, he rushed in to offer what help he could; and as his heart went out in loving concern, and his hands were offered in needed ministries, suddenly there—in those ugly, noisy surroundings—came an assurance of nearness of God such as he had never felt before.

Workers do young persons a disservice who would protect them too carefully from facing evils in the world as they really are; who would fain foist upon the youth their own timidities and unwillingness to serve with full heart. Only as units of study and discussion become *motivation* for action have they served their vital purpose.

Similarly, young persons may be prone to be content with planning worship services of rare beauty—replete with soft candlelight, quiet music, mystic poetry, and the like. And there is a place at times for that which stills and helps one make of one's heart a quiet lake to reflect the Light. But habits of depending upon such settings or of requiring such props can be enervating spiritually. Rather should young persons be challenged strongly to embark upon activities of concern and service (as for example, channels listed in the next-to-last chapter), that they may amidst their work experience a fuller sense of partnership—not only with the Jesus Shepherd of stained-glass window quiet meadows, but rather with the Master Workman as He moves among men!

Less Adult Intrusion, and More Youth Response

When wonder is opening up a new world to young spirits, adults must needs learn when not to intrude. This is one of the hardest lessons of all to learn, especially for the conscientious adult worker eager to fulfill his responsibilities. The teacher who is most aware of God—in work or in worship—will know best when to be silent . . . will recognize the brushing of spirit wings in a group, or in a young person's life.

A group of senior youth had been discussing aspects of the personality of Jesus as suggested by different artists. They had used a few well-chosen pictures. Their teacher, nervously eager to be sure they were all "participating," tried to introduce a controversial issue "simply to get them started discussing," he said. He killed something genuine by cutting off the freshness and newness of their first thinking along lines suggested in this unusual approach. Real "participation" may be inward. It must always be *from the inside out*.

Experiences, if they are real, do not have to be labeled "learning" or "worship" or "service action." Responses do not have to be all of any one kind. Young persons may be truly "participating" in worship or thought while no one breathes a word, or while other things are going on, or while hands are busy at some task. Silence may at times be a most sincere response. A young person may be praying more truly in spirit through silence than when saying words aloud merely for some mistrusting adult's ears.

Some seniors and older youth had driven to an elevation in the foothills of the Rockies in New Mexico, and for their evening meditation one of their number had spoken quietly but earnestly about his commitment to go as a missionary doctor. The sun slipped down, leaving its golden glow. The impact of that boy's sincerity had similarly left a glow upon all hearts. Only the sounds of evening broke the silence—that is, until the impatient counselor thinking evidently that "nothing was happening" began rubbing his hands in overdisplay of zest and said, "Now, let's all pitch in and have a good discussion, what say?" It was like a blow. In a quiet voice the young girl who had been leader that evening said, "Perhaps we can save our thoughts for some future meeting. Suppose we sing together as a prayer the first stanza of 'Dear Lord and Father of Mankind.'" She led a brief benediction and they went home.

But perhaps most workers with youth find themselves praying in anguish that somehow their young people may come to a more reverential spirit; many try earnestly for several weeks to guide a noisome, flighty group to some semblance of quietness, much less worship awareness. Their sincere efforts will someday bear fruit; the contagion of their own spiritual lives will be transmitted perhaps sometime when they are least aware. For all the while, God, too, is working in those young hearts!

XII

CLOSE-UP VIEW OF TEACHER
PREPARATION

*Ye are my witnesses, saith the Lord, and my servants whom I
have chosen: that ye may know and believe me....*
ISAIAH 43:10

Community Church, Yourtown. A new unit is coming for a certain
group of senior young people. It represents a potential "journey of
experience" these young persons may take—never to go back again
to the place where they were before. Every moment of every session
pulses with eternal significance. Staggering are the possibilities for
this unit journey in the lives of these seniors. Staggering are the
possibilities of what may happen to the world through them.

How shall the worker prepare? How avoid pitfalls? How keep
himself from rushing on ahead, lest the feet of his youth never get
started on the path?

To get ready, he gets himself a notebook—a mechanical matter,
perhaps, yet not mechanical in the values it ushers in. Persons have
their own preferences as to size and type of notebooks; the important
thing is that planning be cumulative, and systematic, and useful.

*First Step: The Worker Prepares in Terms of
His Own Spiritual Affirmations*

Throughout his teaching, and now anew at the beginning of a
coming unit, he affirms that he is not teaching alone. The grace of
God is in the process, perchance sometimes in spite of what the
teacher does. Guiding young persons is evangelism in its highest and
perhaps its most lasting form. This particular unit may be "God's
opportunity." The teacher prays that he may in no wise *get in the
way* of the workings of the spirit of the Living God. He seeks guidance, then keeps mind and heart open to receive. He prays for

sensitivity to his young people. Then he rises from his knees to add careful workmanship to his prayers.

Second Step: He Sees the Unit Whole

With what area of youth experience does this unit deal? He looks through the printed material offered, thumbing through the entire unit at once. He visualizes a possible "journey of experience" his young people may take, moving from where they now are in their knowledge and attitudes over to a higher place representing *what they may become*. He holds the printed pages of helps in his hands, realizing that he has here a dynamic potential for youth experiencing.

First he thinks his way through the central idea of the unit before reading. Taking the title and the Scripture references, he asks himself, "What can this topic mean to my Jim, my Sue, my Ann, my Jack?" "Why did the denominational editors and curriculum builders include this unit in just this form at just this time of the year?" "What questions have my group members asked recently that this unit might help to answer?" "Upon what problems of theirs might this material help throw light?" "For what decisions on their part might it bid?" "What possible changes might it make in their living?"

The teacher pauses to make a list of such problems and questions in his notebook, else he will likely forget. These are his "contact points"—between the unit-as-it-is-now-on-paper, and the unit journey the live young persons themselves may take!

He is still not ready to read. "What do I know already about this subject?" "What more do I need to know?" "What do my youth know (perhaps more than I!) about certain aspects of it?" Is there not danger that a worker who uses the same materials year after year may feel that he *knows*? That the ideas become "old stuff" to him? Only as he enters humbly and in learning spirit into each unit as it comes, sensing its potential meaning to the particular group of youth (unlike all others) will he keep a freshness and zest. Yet even with repeated use of materials (as with closely graded materials that are not changed every year), there is an infinitely-beckoning vista for new exploration. The "old, old story" is ever as new as Christmas morning!—That is, if the worker's own spirit is constantly baptized

131

afresh; if he seeks ever to catch the dewy newness of youth's own approach to life.

Prodding a step further into his own experience, he asks himself, "Do I who call myself a follower of the Christ have some personal needs and problems along this line myself? What are they?" Let him be definite, not vague. Let him jot them down that he may seek further help through reading and prayer. The first and foremost step in an adult's preparation for working with young people is his preparation of *himself*.

"Does the central idea of this unit grip and challenge me?" "Does it help me want to live in a more thoroughgoing Christlike way?" "Does it waken me in the middle of the night with its startling implications?" "At what points in my own life might it call for changes— even drastic ones?" If every unit for young people themselves is "for a verdict," and bids for life-changing, what about recommitment first on the part of the teacher?

No one can "interest" young people in something if he himself is not *interested*. Unless a worker himself feels a lump in his throat, unless he himself gets a "whopping big bang" of conviction, let him seek other service in the Vineyard.

Now he reads the unit through. He wants his first introduction to the Big Idea in the unit to be through youth's own eyes in so far as possible; therefore, he reads the pupils' materials first. Then he turns to the teachers' and counselors' helps. At first reading, he will probably not go into minute detail. He will give more attention later.

Now he wants to get the direction of the unit as a whole. Some can scan so as not to miss any significant point. The time thus taken will be time saved in the long run, for he can then "mull over" the ideas while going about his daily chores. One's best insights often come "out of the corner of one's eye" while doing other things. Thus preparation time is extended. One teacher says that she spends two hours in preparation for each Sunday, but many hours all week in actual preparation while doing her daily tasks.

Third Step: He Prepares in Terms of the Individuals in His Group

Even as he reads, the teacher sees the faces of individual young persons superimposed upon the printed words on paper. Some are laughing, some glum, some perplexed. Steadfastly, he focuses upon them. Is Randy restless? Did the teacher by chance see the clever cartoon Randy drew of him last Sunday? Has the teacher sufficient sense of humor to overlook the point of the cartoon and realize that Randy has here a rare gift of humor and artistic talent that can benefit others if developed? Is Edith stupid? Or is it that her personality is locked behind doors of timidity and fear of ridicule? Has the teacher by chance heard her sing?

The teacher who has kept a secret notebook about members of his group will refer to it often as he prepares . . . as he refers continually to it in his prayers.

Fourth Step: He Prepares in Terms of the Relation of This Unit to the Community and World Situation, and Its Impingement Upon Young Personalities

What do the headlines say? What events are of import to the young people themselves? Which affect them personally? Which are on the periphery of their awareness? About which are they emotionally involved? How can a teacher take hold at such points? Which of the events or problems furnish leads for stimulating interest in the area of the unit? Are certain problems so immediate as to suggest postponing the unit, so as to allow for consideration of them while the interest is hot? In what way does the present community and world situation affect the *purposes* for the unit? What further possibilities for youth action (beyond those normally included in the unit) are suggested by the present situation? What are some implications for the Christian living of young persons? What decisions on their part are called for? About what clusters of concern might these young persons engage in further prayer?

Fifth Step: He Prepares by Using the Bible

The teacher should *use*, not merely refer to, his Bible in making his preparation. Let him look up the Scripture references and possibly find others in addition to those listed in the printed helps. Let him take time to think of some possible ways these passages may be

133

used by his young people. What is more embarrassing and less meaningful to a group than for individuals to stumble through a Scripture reading which neither leader nor group have read beforehand? The worker's own Bible should be his constant companion, the teacher's teacher.

When looking up references given, let him familiarize himself with the context. Any difficult words to pronounce? Let him look them up (he will not tell his young people, but assist them in finding and practicing correct pronunciation). Let him decide whether certain passages are to be used informally (helping young people get at the facts) or devotionally. There is a difference.

Sixth Step: He Gathers Additional Materials

From the workers' helps, the teacher may discover that pictures, other books, films or such further aids might prove helpful. Some nonadventurous teachers stop there, but such a reaction is shortsighted. For all denominational helps are limited in space. Although the basic necessary helps are always there, references are included as to additional materials such as may be welcomed by the young people. Public school, community, or pastor's libraries may have the books suggested. Addresses are often given to which letters may be written for free pictures, maps, pamphlets, and other aids. Ministers may assist in securing what is needed. Naturally, to gather materials one must start several weeks in advance; one cannot wait until the Saturday evening before! Young people themselves can write the letters, make posters, prepare exhibits, borrow books (and take responsibility for returning!).

Seventh Step: He Prepares, With the Help of Some Young People, the Room Arrangement and Setting

The materials to be used are gotten together. Young people may help arrange attractively, or in such a way as to create curiosity or stimulate interest. Some church meeting rooms, unfortunately, do not lend themselves to much change in arrangement. Probably they were built without adequate knowledge of or attention to the educational process. At least chairs can be arranged for fellowship: in a
134

circle if possible, or around tables for research activities. At least the room can be clean and orderly. Tools (blackboard, chalk, or newsprint with black crayon and other materials) should be made ready.

Eighth Step: He Outlines Purposes for This Particular Unit

Good teachers teach "for a verdict." Good counselors with evening sessions hope that something will happen in these meetings besides merely "putting on a program" and having the group feel entertained. The worker, and such committees of young persons as plan with him, may regard themselves as John the Baptist, to "prepare the way"—that the living Truth may find channel to young hearts and through them to others.

What is the specific aim or what are the aims for this unit? What does the teacher hope will help youth most? What changes does he hope may take place in the thinking of the young people? In their emotional responses? In their appreciations and sympathies? In their worship life? In their strength of will for meeting specific temptations? What youth-felt problems may this unit help solve? Having charted aims and held these up in prayer, the teacher will then approach each moment as if he *expected something to happen!*

Ninth Step: He Sketches Out Tentative Plans

Not to plan is fatal. To follow a plan is fatal. The more thoroughly the adult worker plans, the more freely he and his youth can depart from the details of his plans, moving ever toward the goal of the unit. Secure because he has thought through possible activities of learning, and various aspects of the Big Idea of the unit, he can relax and be alert to his group in a way that would be impossible if he were uncertain as to next possible turns. Without careful plans, he and his group may be at the mercy of whims and fancies; or they may follow slavishly the pattern laid down in the printed pages.

To plan does not imply blind obedience to that plan. Rather, the worker starts a process of continuous, flexible, evolving planning. After the first few minutes of the first session, when youth's own interests have been challenged, they themselves will share in choos-

135

ing activities and in further planning. Having planned in terms of the unit-as-a-whole, the adult leader sees several possible paths the group journey may take toward the goals. He is ready, now, to go with his young people on any of these. Thus he can be serene as he meets with them. That attitude on his part causes them to feel more at ease with him, and responses will flow the more freely.

Tenth Step: He Plans Ways of Encouraging Youth Participation

Now that he has saturated himself with the helps in the printed materials and other sources, the worker has courage to put them aside. He is to be custodian of a living process, not of materials only.

Clearly, quietly, he tries to visualize the situation he will face in the first session. He gives himself a "preview." He sees his young people, stepping for an hour or so out of their stream of daily activities into the church building—yet not out of the stream, for they bring it with them. They are *living* in the church hour as truly as when they play their games on the ball court or exchange confidences over a soda. "We learn what we live." What will this group be *living*, as they come for this first session?

The teacher, recalling individual interests, will be prepared to suggest several possible choices of activities through which the young persons may work toward the unit goal. He is ready to go along with them, whichever paths they choose.

He reminds himself that he is not so important as he might like to think. He cannot *make* these young folks interested. He can only invite. He can provide to some extent at the church a "growth environment," stimulating their curiosity, prodding their interests, calling forth their eagerness to do for themselves.

Interest may be likened to the doorway pictured in Holman Hunt's "Light of the World." The Figure is at the door knocking; but He cannot force His way in. The latch is on the inside. Each young person must *want* to open the door of his interest from the inside. No amount of bombardment by adult will force its opening.

Are there no appeals a teacher may use? No clues? Yes, many!

1. *Sense of felt need.* That need must be felt by the young person
136

himself, not as an echo of what he feels the adult wants him to feel.

2. *Desire to overcome some obstacle or find a solution to some problem.* The problem, too, must be the young person's own. If it is not already so, how can the teacher help him feel its urgency, and its impingement upon himself? Workers may give thought to such questions.

3. *Relation to some already-formed interest.* The worker's knowledge (and notes) about the hobbies of his young people come to his rescue at this point.

4. *Natural curiosity.* Growing persons have a fund of native curiosity. Within most units are some fascinating possibilities inviting exploration. The worker seeks to ferret out those that would awaken curiosity.

5. *Further ideas along the line of some previously happy experience.* Persons tend to want to repeat experiences that have brought pleasure and satisfaction, and not to repeat those that have resulted otherwise.

6. *Lure of new adventure.* Activities sometimes prove a good starting point; intermediates, especially, rise to the pull of something that looks like "fun to do."

7. *Contagion of someone else's enthusiasm.* The teacher's own genuine interest will attract. But youth are wise to synthetic enthusiasm. Interest must be challenged on deeper levels if it is to be sustained. The interest of one or two members (if they happen to be natural leaders in the group) will provide contagion for the rest.

Whatever the appeal, it must reach the emotions if it is to obtain response in action. There is a vast amount of inertia in youth. They may perceive with their minds that they need help. But this is not enough to prod them to wide-awake interest and action. Their imaginations must be kindled, their latent energies "sparked."

Many good teachers report that a sizable percentage of their total time for unit preparation (some say up to 90 per cent) is spent on this point: "How awaken interest?" Once those doorways are open from the inside, the young persons will embark with zest upon the adventure the unit promises.

Never Fully Prepared

The worker has now taken certain steps of preparation, although probably no *good* teacher ever felt himself to be fully prepared. The more he senses the dangerous opportunity before him, the more frightened and humble he becomes. His fear may well be lest he not be afraid *enough!* For guiding young lives is like handling high voltage powers.

The less adequate the teacher feels, the more he will rely upon God. Good teaching means God-teaching: of persons through persons, that all may find the Person.

Next Steps: Youth Themselves Set up Purposes, Participate in Planning and Carrying Through Their Activities of Learning

The next chapter will focus on young persons themselves awakening to possibilities, forming committees and otherwise working zestfully toward goals they have helped set up; and judging at the close of their unit journey whether they have traveled over the territory they set for themselves, and what they need now to do to follow through from their decisions into action.

Closing Step: The Adult Worker Evaluates Alone, After Each Unit

"Alone with his thoughts" on a Sunday afternoon, the adult worker goes back over the steps he made in preparation, the various sessions of the unit, and the activities through which the young people participated, including the summary they have made and their evaluation.

Did the young people feel they accomplished their purposes?

Does he, the teacher, feel that together they arrived at their chosen goal? On what evidence?

He should be able to see farther than the young people (else why should they need an adult helper?). He realizes that real growth may not have taken place all at once. Some hidden seeds may bring forth fruit years to come, for better or for worse. These he cannot measure in his Sunday afternoon soliloquy. He can only trust.

But he can think back over his own part in the process. He can ask himself realistically at what points he might have done a better job as adult friend: *perhaps done better by doing less and letting them do more!*

Could I have made a better beginning approach in the first moments?

Did I help them form purposes of their own? Or was I too easily satisfied when they assented to *my* purpose, and chose the activities I had in mind?

Did I offer suggestions tactfully, and in such manner as to leave the way open for them to choose freely?

Did I contribute all I could to help them have a happy, friendly group atmosphere? Should I have tried harder to win Judy into the circle? Was I sufficiently sensitive to each individual?

Could I have met John's sudden, off-the-subject question more wisely?

Did I focus too much attention upon the activities themselves? When the young people got busy in their work, did I let them lose sight at any point of the reasons back of the activities?

Did I try sufficiently to help each individual feel that he was needed by the group as a whole, and that he could share or bring up problems as he wished?

Did we find opportunities for varying forms of individual expression (including some not involving speaking, so as to give the more timid ones their chance)?

Did we try to do too many things? Could more have been accomplished had we narrowed our efforts more carefully to the mainline problems? Would we have had a deeper experience of discovery had we tried to get over less material?

Did the group have sufficient time? Or did they feel "too rushy"?

Were discussion periods helpful, or did we sometimes waste time? At what instances should I have been more alert as leader?

Are the group members growing in their courtesy to one another?

Was there a sense of our relationship to the larger world?

Was there a sense of relationship with God and His purposes throughout? Are there evidences that any members of the group have clearer ideas now as to what it means to follow Jesus' way? Was some new commitment made? Some renewal of ideals?

Is the teacher himself a better Christian, as the result of this unit? In what ways has it helped him grow? What weaknesses in his own living has it revealed to him? To what new decisions has it led him? What has it meant in his prayer life? In his social attitudes? In his willingness to further dedicate his time, energy, and money to the purposes and will of God?

XIII

PURPOSEFUL PARTICIPATION
BY YOUTH

*See, I have this day set thee over the nations and over the king-
doms, . . . to build, and to plant.* JEREMIAH 1:10

Summary of Principles Thus Far

We have seen how young persons may share actively and joyously
in building, with their adult leaders in the church, a year's calendar
of Sunday school and evening meeting units and other activities.
We have noted that this experience of *planning* is itself an aid for
wholesome growth. We have watched the adult worker's function as
that of helping these young persons identify and crystallize their
problems, think carefully what interests claim them, decide what
dreams move them. Instruments such as checklists, and notes on
questions raised spontaneously serve well in this process of planning
which should be continuous, year-round. At each step of the way,
rapport between young people and adult leader is essential.

We have watched young persons, once they know what their needs
and interests are, looking ahead at denominational yearbooks, noting
coming units along the lines of these needs and interests. Thus a
calendar is built, following rather closely the framework of the dated
units but allowing for such flexibility as will enable the particular
youth in a given local church to feel that their specific needs are being
met. Units are charted into the calendar in a careful, well-balanced
plan using the spiritually vitamin-packed menu of church helps for
the age group.

Now the youth can feel that the plans are *theirs,* and they will
chart in further related activities such as recreational events correlated
with the emphases in the units, projects of serving and giving, and
the like. They can invite friends to come, for "we'll be talking about

141

such-and-such." So carefully have curriculum planners worked that almost all possible interests of an age level will be found reflected in the year's (or at least in the cycle's) offering of units. The value in a local group's planning and calendar-building is psychological. The situation—in the eyes of the young persons themselves—has shifted from one where they come blindly to Sunday school not knowing what the lesson is going to be about and depending wholly on the adult, to one where they themselves are not only "in" on the planning but responsible with the adult.

No longer, then, are printed materials something to be opened at the time of the class or evening session, with a more or less mechanical following paragraph by paragraph. Rather, here are interesting thoughts from others dealing with the very questions and problems the young people have raised. Publicity committees can plan clever posters, call attention to the subjects under discussion in a variety of attractive ways.

We turn now to ask how a group of intermediates, or seniors, or older youth participate with the adult worker in a specific unit in the Sunday school or evening session. We have seen in the preceding chapter the adult worker himself preparing for a coming unit.

Where in the process do the young people come in? Is the adult worker supposed to do all the planning for the Sunday school units, trying of course to elicit some participation at least verbally from the young people when they get there? Are the youth themselves supposed to do all planning for the evening meeting? The answer to both questions is an emphatic "No!" As seen earlier, *whenever* a group of young persons with adult helper get together, the basic principles for good learning should be followed—morning, evening, any time. There must be worked out a "working relationship" for each age level. Younger youth need far more adult help than older ones. But for *both* morning and evening units, with the adult worker doing first some necessary basic over-all preparing, the young people (at *each* age level) come in on the *planning*, the *carrying-through*, and the *evaluating*; then the adult worker evaluates in an over-all way.

The Group Members and Their Leader Decide on
Purposes and Make Plans

An evening society of seniors and older youth was about to begin a new unit on "Jesus and the Problems of Life." The key to this unit is effort to interpret certain of Jesus' mainline teachings in terms of present youth-felt problems. A committee of the young people had been busily making preparations with their counselor; they had "caught" the core idea of the unit; they had thought carefully how to help the others awaken to the need of putting Jesus' teachings to work in their problems of living. The committee decided *not* to begin with a routinelike series of talks. They realized that the need was first to prod and stimulate the group members until they *wanted* to discover what Jesus' teachings for their problems were . . .

And so on the opening evening of the unit, when the members gathered, what did they find had happened to their meeting room? Instead of the usual rows of chairs, there were little informal clusters of chairs in corners, and tables in the center with many newspapers and pairs of scissors around. The committee members suggested that for ten minutes persons clip articles illustrating the following of Jesus' way, or not-following. The latter pile grew the faster. There was much conversation, and a growing tone of seriousness. What *did* Jesus teach about such-and-such a problem? These youth were thinking. To be sure, the floor became littered; one of the hoary church fathers dropping in might have been inclined to sigh about youth's noisome activity instead of sitting still and listening. But something was happening *inside* them. There is such a thing as creative litter! Soon they were listing questions as to what Jesus did teach, applicable for today.

(Had one glanced in the printed materials from which these ideas were taken, he would have found a list of questions ready-made. But how much more meaningful to this particular group if *they themselves* are wondering, and if they put questions in their own words! The committee was alert to fill in areas they omitted, thus using the printed materials as an aid.) Soon all had found places in the

143

little circles of chairs, using their Bibles and looking up various references for Jesus' teachings the committee gave them. Each group would have something to share with the total group when the chairs were drawn into the larger circle later. Much would be accomplished, digging into the very heart of the unit, because the members were stimulated first to have a *purpose* in finding what Jesus taught.

A group started a unit on vocations. But sadly, instead of helping them first to decide upon their *purposes*—what they wished to decide about vocations and why—the teacher began feverishly lecturing with miscellaneous information about miscellaneous vocations. There was a muchness of material, but a minimum of interest. Some of the information the boys and girls already had from school units. What they needed from their church was some criterion for choosing. Had the teacher thought more carefully, and had she been more familiar with what they were learning in school, she should have given focus and awakened the members to want to have standards for deciding. They themselves could have supplied information, or worked in little research or interview committees to find and bring. This teacher had prepared, but in a materials-centered sort of way; obviously, she had thought of teaching as telling. But had she been more concerned to help them *learn,* she would have started perhaps with some little episodes showing persons facing decisions, or maybe with questions stimulating other questions on their part. A committee might have prepared a little dramatized interview bringing out the question, "*Why* choose this or that vocation?"

An intermediate class is beginning a new unit on the life of Jesus. Is their teacher guiding their inquisitiveness, their delight in the colorful and the dramatic, their eagerness to work with their hands, or their latent capacity for hero worship—so that they will first *want* to discover more about this Life? Sadly, she is not . . .

She has opened the quarterly in the same way she usually does. She bids her pupils do the same (teaching thereby what? Unthinking compliance with authority, perhaps?). "Mary, you take the first Scripture verse, Jim the next, and so around the line." (Should not their Bibles themselves be used, and should not the Scripture readings be looked up reverently and read more thoughtfully—perhaps later in the session when interest has been generated, when they have a *purpose* in discovering what the Bible says?)

"Now, let's get down to the lesson." (Does the teacher mean that the Scripture has had nothing to do with "the lesson"?) "It says here . . ." (Obviously the teacher has not prepared; the intermediates are aware; she is not bluffing them.) What possible *purpose* might the boys and girls have for finding "what it says here"? For listening?

Suppose that in her preparation, she had centered first at the very heart of this unit: the amazing heroism, wonder, power, fearlessness, and beauty of this Life. The unit was to be a kind of "introduction," drawing together in connected story the many episodes these boys and girls had already learned about earlier as children; but now as intermediates they could "see the Life whole" in a fuller way. The need would be to help awaken them to *want* to try to see Jesus' life whole.

Perhaps she could have secured a meaningful picture, or maybe more than one. Denominational houses have beautiful but inexpensive pictures, worthy and carefully chosen. Rather than beginning the session in a mechanical way, perhaps the teacher could have placed the picture against fitting background; and in the opening moments all could have sat quietly thinking, seeking to imagine how He must have really looked. ("But will intermediates be quiet?" some teacher may ask. Yes! —If they have *purpose*. And thinking and imagining can be *active* stillness!) Intermediates have active imaginations once given wings; they can almost "see" Him moving amidst people, some of whom were their own age. (It was a real place in a real world, and these were real people with whom He associated. The startling *reality* of this Life is often missed by mechanical procedures like "reading around," or "it says here.")

The familiar words of the hymn, "I think when I read that sweet story of old," might be shared by the committee of intermediates that has assisted the teacher in making preparation for this first session. What questions would these intermediates have wanted to ask Him, had they been in those crowds? What questions *did* people ask Him? *Why?*

Suppose the intermediates had begun entering vicariously through
145

their imaginations into even one of the scenes . . . already the door would have been opened to new vistas of discovery . . . they would be off to find out more about this amazing Life—*for themselves!* They would have purpose.

It is important that purposes awakened in young people be *worthy!* Suppose Johnny determines fiercely to himself, "I'm going to have the best-looking workbook!" And later, because of his preoccupation with selfish interests, he refuses to help another member of the group. No matter if the "lesson" about which he is writing in his workbook is on brotherhood, Johnny is practicing something else. One learns what one practices, according to one's purpose.

We throw back another curtain. This time, what is taking place is not according to a planned unit, but the young people are learning just the same! The senior department is having its annual election of officers. The very air is heated. With all the fervor (and some of the skill) of embryonic politicians, each "side" argues for its representatives. There is much "purpose," to be sure. But is it worthy? Is it making for Christian attitudes and practices? An important function of the adult worker in such situations is to foresee potentially harmful learnings, and if possible through tactful planning ahead with the young people, to help them purpose to practice Christian dealings, even with one another in all situations, even elections.

Once a group of young persons *wants* to get somewhere on a problem, such as the key problem of a new unit, then their next step is to plan how to get there! The adult worker in his preliminary preparation, as we have seen, has noted perhaps a number of different pathways for youth choice, all of which pathways lead toward the goal of the unit.

The young people themselves can visualize the journey opening out before them. Just where *does* this unit lead? What steps will be needed to arrive at the solution of the problem, or to find the information, or to develop the attitudes suggested?

Material may be offered in the curriculum helps for say, five sessions (or more, or less, depending on the bigness of the idea in the unit). Why not lump together all this session time into one whole, and plan just how to use it most wisely—maybe not necessarily trying to "cover" exactly what is dated for each successive Sunday, but seeking to get at the heart of the unit, the core idea. Looking ahead and budgeting time, so much for this committee report, so much for that activity, etc., is valuable practice for youth as for their adult workers. Question may be asked, "But would valuable time in a church school class itself be taken up, with this exploration and youth planning?" Yes! For important in their learnings is practice in planning, and in following through toward worthy goals! And only thus, as *they* have purpose, and as *they* help make plans for arriving at the purpose, will the learning be *theirs!*

An intermediate group was taking up a unit on "Religion and the World's Work." They thumbed through the material offered for all the Sundays in the unit. They noted that here were several major vocational areas, arranged one to a Sunday. However, as they faced their own needs to know how to choose according to the Christian way, they decided to spend two sessions discussing *how* to choose; then they would all volunteer for different work groups, finding information on all these areas simultaneously for two weeks; then they would spend the remainder of their time bringing their findings together, and looking at the vocations in the light of the conclusions they had reached about *how* to choose. Rather than a slavish following of dates, they were making their unit study an adventure. The work groups used the printed materials, each on their chosen area; the sharing-time brought the information before all.

Members of the group, then, can volunteer for certain responsibilities. (How much more natural, and more valuable for their growth than merely being asked to "take part" by the adult or by a committee even of their own group!) When they have purpose, and when they know that a certain phase of the unit is depending on them alone, they will use the printed materials voluntarily. (How much better than the adult assigning mechanically as "home work" and lamenting that they do not "study"!)

A rough tentative plan is made, then, for the entire unit. As it moves along, changes and adaptations can be made. The very process

147

of doing so is valuable experience in group work. Only through practice do young persons learn the gives-and-takes of good Christian fellowship.

In a unit on "Our Diminishing World," a senior group staged a United Nations conference table, outlining carefully the international problems to be brought up and their points for discussion as a Christian group.

An older youth group working on "Jesus' Way Our Way" dramatized scenes in their own lives in duplicate: first, as the scenes would appear if they followed purely selfish motives; second, as they would appear if they followed Christian motives.

An intermediate group summarized their mission study on Africa through setting up an "African Village," illustrating various aspects of village life including the mission work about which they had learned.

The activities themselves are not the important thing, but rather the experiences the young persons are having as they work them out, and the way they relate their findings to their ongoing purposes for better living.

Choice Is Made of Modes of Learning in Harmony With Purposes

As they gain experience in setting up purposes, planning steps for arriving, then evaluating their work, young people soon discover that some types of activities seem to fit best with certain purposes. They learn to suit methods to needs. (Sometimes adult workers need to learn this way of evaluating possible activities, also.) They discover when it would be fitting to have discussion; when such would *not* be fitting but would lead away from what they wish to accomplish at the time, when possibly committee work or quiet meditation or other media would be more meaningful.

Young people and their adult workers, as they plan together, will probably discover that usually a given unit—if they focus carefully on the core idea at the heart of it and think how to arrive at this idea in the most direct way—calls for one major or key type of learning activity. For a problem-solving unit, discussion is probably the key method. For a missions unit bidding for deepening of appre-
148

ciations, the use of a film or of flat pictures may be a key method. For an informational unit, activities of research or interview, possibly trips and the like may be needed. Common sense suggests what methods would be most fruitful, keeping always the specific purpose of the unit itself in clear view. Thus, both the young people and their adult worker will avoid the pitfall of going off onto tangents, or attempting too many unrelated or merely peripheral activities. Variety is not to be sought merely as an end in itself. It comes as a by-product of true-focused, goal-conscious planning. For the units in each year's cycle will offer variety, both as to subject matter and as to key methods.

A word of warning may be in order. Young people tend, in the first fresh blush of enthusiasm, to attempt more than they can follow through. The adult worker can guide them tactfully to narrow the scope of their plans, and to consider exactly what would be involved in completing any activity they propose to attempt.

Some groups warm up slowly. Two or three sessions may be needed at the beginning to generate interest, set up purposes, and get under way. Once the momentum is up, however, perhaps they can work more rapidly through the remainder of the material than the dates would suggest. It sometimes happens that a group is not ready to leave a unit topic on the date specified; rather than leave a problem in a state of confusion, would it not be better for them to stick with it until ready to move to the next? Better that young persons have one deep, meaningful experience with one idea than take a hop-skip-and-jump over the surface of many!

How, then, may group members with their adult leader know what activities or methods would prove most helpful in achieving their goals? For each given unit, they would find key suggestions in the pupils' and teachers' materials. The following analysis of some possible activities or modes of learning may furnish a guide. By no means is this list of activities exhaustive. The teacher (and possibly the young persons themselves in the Sunday school class or evening fellowship) will think of other ideas along similar lines that lead in the desired directions.

1. WHEN THERE IS NEED FOR SUCH ACTIVITIES AS WILL HELP STIMULATE INTEREST, AROUSE CURIOSITY, OR ORIENT YOUNG PERSONS INTO AWARENESS OF A PROBLEM—

   a. Questions. The adult worker or youth committee in previous preparation may list some questions to stimulate thinking. These may be arranged in true-false fashion if desired. Members themselves should be encouraged to ask questions. A "wonder list" may be compiled, with the total group co-operating. Such activities particularly fitting at outset of an informational unit.

   b. Use of pictures (flat pictures, cuttings from magazines, denominational picture sets) to stimulate interest and prompt questions; if facilities afford, projected pictures may be chosen and used to serve similar purpose.

   c. Use of models, curios, exhibits, costumes.

   d. The telling of a story, or of a number of brief episodes to awaken within the group a sense of urgency for tackling the problem at hand or finding the answers.

   e. Excursions to museums, churches, synagogues, farms, woods, industries, and the like.

   f. Group reading of a drama that opens up the problem.

   g. Group reading of a portion of Scripture that opens up the problem.

   h. Etc.

2. WHEN THERE IS NEED FOR ACTIVITIES THROUGH WHICH INFORMATION CAN BE SECURED, ARRANGED, AND INTERPRETED—

   a. Reading, individually or in groups. Recommended resources are always suggested in denominational teachers' and counselors' helps, but the basic reading resource will be the printed materials for the unit. Public libraries, the pastor's library, and other sources may be visited. Careful reading of Scripture references, with individual thought and group discussion of meanings, should be considered a high privilege and not merely duty.

b. Use of pictures of various kinds—pictures, for this use, through which information is gained (as for example, regarding life in Palestine or in a mission station).

c. Use of maps, graphs, charts, and the like.

d. Visits, trips, surveys—with careful setting up of the questions before going, notes on information gained, and evaluation after returning.

e. Interviews or bringing of resource persons into the group, that questions may be asked of them according to the group's need.

f. Use of radio and other current news sources.

g. Use of recordings such as documentaries, imparting information.

h. Etc.

3. WHEN THERE IS NEED FOR EXPERIENCES THAT WILL HELP ENLARGE SYMPATHIES AND DEEPEN APPRECIATIONS—

a. Stories—told by youth themselves, after careful preparation; or told by the adult worker, or by resource persons, or on recordings. Selection may be made first of all from that which is offered in the printed helps for the unit, or from other recommended sources. Choice should be made carefully in terms of this unique purpose, and the telling should be done with genuine sincerity so that the contagion of emotional identification can take place.

b. Drama—walking rehearsals of recommended plays (possibly using only chosen excerpts so as to conserve time); group reading, as of Scripture scenes; or impromptu acting out of ideas, or "role-playing" of problem episodes that awaken awareness of needs faced by others.

c. Visual helps—including use of costumes, pictures, films, curios, and the like. Selection would be made with care in terms of those few helps that would best serve to provide

151

background, and help members transport themselves in imaginations to the land under consideration, or feel a one-ness with the peoples.

d. Music—live or recorded. Folk songs sometimes help establish rapport between peoples of widely varying backgrounds.

e. Games. Probably if games of other peoples are to be played, or menus sampled, such would be done at a fun-and-fellowship occasion that may be scheduled as a part of this particular unit.

f. Creative writing—encouraging the young people to express in their own native ways, such awareness as they have come to feel.

g. Worship—not just a "program about" a subject; but a sincere God-centered effort to extend love and concern and perhaps intercessory prayer.

h. Etc.

4. WHEN THERE IS NEED FOR WAYS OF EXPRESSING YOUTH'S OWN THOUGHTS, OR FOR RECORDING OR ILLUSTRATING THEIR FINDINGS, OR FOR MEDIA FOR SHARING WITH OTHERS—

a. The making of posters, murals, friezes, scrapbooks, newspapers, maps, exhibits, and the like—through which to record or convey to others, basic findings the young people themselves have made in a particular unit.

b. The use of a dramatic way to bring to others (such as a parents' group) the ideas discovered. Variations of drama may include puppets or marionettes, pantomime, radio drama.

c. Verse speaking or group reading of key thoughts—originally put together by the young people themselves as their summary of their findings.

d. Poetry writing, hymn writing, script writing, or other forms of creative writing to summarize findings.

e. Artistic recording of findings: as for example in murals

(with different individuals or groups working on different panels simultaneously, possibly); illuminated manuscripts; sculpture (potato, soap, clay); paintings; pastels; cartoon-type strips.

f. Diary, logbook, or mimeographed record of findings.

g. Simulated stained-glass window in which key ideas have been translated into appropriate symbolism.

h. Exhibits arranged for open house for parents or others.

i. Litany for use in worship. Other worship aids, such as prayers, stories, or meditations prepared by the young persons themselves from the information and inspiration the unit has brought.

5. WHEN THERE IS NEED FOR METHODS THROUGH WHICH YOUNG PERSONS CAN SOLVE PROBLEMS—

a. Group discussion (including variations such as panels with prepared suggestions on certain aspects of the problem; "buzz" groups each working on some aspect of the problem; Socratic dialogue; "staging" scenes where the problem is faced (this may become role playing, and possibly prove therapeutic in itself as individuals are encouraged to act out unafraid certain roles of others who are causing them difficulties).

b. Trips, surveys, interviews, and the like to ferret out information needed for the solving of the problem.

c. Use of a film or recording, either for setting the problem squarely before the group, or for suggesting possible solutions; any such material should be thoroughly evaluated afterward.

d. Try-out of tentative solutions—perhaps dramatically first, in a series of "pre-view" episodes.

e. Decision making. Discussion, no doubt, but possibly some moments of silence for individuals to think through to their own personal conclusions. If desired, a worship setting may be arranged in an upper room or chapel, and members may kneel for prayer individually or as a group. Or a fellow-

153

ship circle at the close of the discussion may offer an opportunity for individuals to express through testimonials or prayer the conclusions to which they have come, and what they feel they should do, with God's help, in following through in their lives.

f. Etc.

(Immediately it will be noted that under several of the headings above, similar activities or methods are listed; but the focus would be in terms of the *purpose* to be served.)

6. WHEN THE PURPOSE IS CHRISTIAN SERVICE ACTION—

a. *Christian service action in the area of churchmanship—*

(1) Prayer.

(2) Regular and prompt participation in church worship.

(3) Wholehearted participation in all church activities.

(4) Welcome activities for strangers.

(5) Giving of money.

(6) Doing well each responsibility undertaken.

(7) Finding out what service activities are being planned by other groups in the church and joining forces with them.

(8) Studying the work of church boards and organizations.

(9) Improving the church grounds and building.

(10) Participating in youth choir.

(11) Being an active member of the youth fellowship—helping in all activities; practicing friendliness; striving to reach unreached.

(12) Equipping a game room in the church.

(13) Assisting the pastor by distributing materials, flowers, bulletins; making telephone calls; running errands.

(14) Issuing invitations to strangers.

(15) Drawing or mimeographing a map of the community giving directions to the church, and distributing to strangers.

(16) Visiting shut-ins; doing kindly deeds for them such as reading to them or bringing music to them.

(17) Making posters to announce special occasions.

(18) Volunteering to drive cars to pick up shut-ins or others who could not otherwise attend. Baby-sitting for parents to go to activities in the church.

(19) Purchasing an individual communion set for the pastor's use with the shut-ins and hospitalized. Furnishing recordings of services or music to go to these persons.

(20) Assisting with secretarial work of the church.

(21) Holding services in institutions.

(22) Writing up stories of church events for local newspapers or church papers.

(23) Preparing some little-used room in the church as a chapel for individual prayer and small services.

(24) Keeping the church building clean and attractive.

(25) Caring for church hymnals and Bibles and books of worship.

(26) Providing flowers.

(27) Starting a costume wardrobe, collecting and classifying costumes for different types of dramatic productions.

(28) Starting an art library—sorting, mounting, and filing pictures for ready use for teaching and worship purposes.

(29) Making movable screens for church school rooms, particularly for children's rooms.

(30) Assisting children's workers (under their supervision) in storytelling, preparing equipment, gathering materials, and caring for children.

(31) Maintaining fellowship with persons away from the home church, through letters, bulletins, recordings, devotional aids, newssheets.

(32) Faithfulness as a group in participating in the worship and general work of the church.

(33) Etc.

b. *Reaching unreached persons—*

   (1) Finding who and where the unreached are. Making a house-to-house canvass or other type of community or school survey.

   (2) Publicizing church events (through personal word, telephone, posters, newspapers, bulletins, radio).

   (3) Making provision for recreation regularly for youth and possibly also children's and/or adult groups, with a variety of activities including the quiet and the active to appeal to different tastes and moods.

   (4) Making provision for transportation of unreached persons.

   (5) Co-operating with youth fellowships of other churches and faiths.

   (6) Providing for services in closed churches.

   (7) Starting neighborhood prayer groups.

   (8) Starting outpost Sunday schools (under supervision of trained adult workers).

   (9) Developing an "enlistment" service to help newcomers find niches for participation.

   (10) Providing a lounge in the church building for reading, writing, or listening to music and for meeting friends under worthy auspices—for individuals who have no such places to go.

   (11) Visiting unreached persons in homes; assuring them of sincere, friendly interest, following up by bringing them to church activities.

   (12) Arranging outdoor sing on Sunday afternoon in summer, especially for unchurched people, or in sections where such opportunities for friendly participation are rarely offered.

   (13) Arranging neighborhood gatherings for unchurched people to meet with friendly church people—for candymaking, packing boxes for relief, preparing for Christmas, etc.

(14) Caroling—not alone at Christmas but possibly at other times as well.

c. *Activities for building brotherhood and world friendship—*

(1) Using special missions materials in denominational and interdenominational publications (units, stories, activity ideas, party suggestions, music, drama).

(2) Providing bibliographies of missionaries and peace-makers who have worked for brotherhood.

(3) Encouraging hobbies that help to build world-mindedness, such as pen pals, stamp collecting, language study, making or collecting dolls of the nations, trips.

(4) Setting up an "overseas workshop," a place where youth can meet to mend clothes, collect goods for relief, repair and make needed items.

(5) Securing for showing among church people visuals or recordings to help deepen concern for others and build world-mindedness.

(6) Inviting persons from other countries and missionaries within reach to counsel with the young people about world relations and possibly vocational missions work.

(7) Setting up a world friendship library or corner or shelf in youth room, or somewhere in the church, or in a basement.

(8) Securing the interest of librarian of public library in arranging a special section or shelf of books dealing with international questions.

(9) Getting in touch with commissions on world peace of the denomination for up-to-the-minute suggestions and materials, such as radio scripts that can be used to build confidence and inspire peace action among the masses.

(10) Securing informational materials, including visual and auditory materials, from United Nations and possibly its branches such as UNESCO. Forming

United Nations club for securing needed information and discussing and disseminating it.

(11) Starting personal campaign to rid one's own speech of slurring words or phrases or jokes ridiculing other people.

(12) Generally living as if all were one brotherhood, speaking that way, thinking that way, praying that way.

(13) Etc.

d. *Christian service action in lifting moral standards—*

(1) Seeing what recreational facilities and guidance are offered in the community to give youth from lower economic levels opportunities for fun and fellowship under worthy auspices, and fostering higher ideals within them.

(2) Getting the facts as to attitudes and practices of youth in the community, schools, etc., as to cheating, stealing, boy-girl friendships, gambling, drinking, use of narcotics.

(3) Calling together for consultation those likely to be most concerned and capable of offering help (church groups, civic agencies, character-building agencies, parents).

(4) Making the total church program for youth so alive that it will help attract and hold the interest of unreached young persons; offering them jobs to do when they come so that they will feel needed, and thus gain foothold in becoming better selves; surrounding them with wholesome group relationships, strengthening their ideals; guiding them in understanding better Jesus' teachings, and leading them to commitment.

(5) Etc.

e. *Christian service action in the local community—*

(1) Arousing interest in a community-wide recreation program for children, youth, and adults (including

hobbies, crafts, outdoor activities, hikes, nature lore, folk games, other games, music, drama, intercultural festivals).

(2) Working in institutions (typing, general work, leading games or crafts, playing piano, assisting with children, telling stories, coaching drama).

(3) Conducting a Sunday afternoon sing each week.

(4) Growing flowers.

(5) Supplying reading materials to jails and other institutions.

(6) Helping harvest or gather perishable crops.

(7) Having a "Lord's Acre" project.

(8) Co-operating in a community survey.

(9) Presenting plays or visual aids dealing with social problems.

(10) Supporting a community project, such as a milk fund for babies (perhaps doing without refreshments at youth meetings, and giving the money that would otherwise have been spent).

(11) Investigating the treatment of criminals and delinquents—particularly of the younger ones—in the community.

(12) Working to overcome juvenile delinquency.

(13) Visiting the jails and detention homes and holding services.

(14) Analyzing the liquor problem in the community and organizing strategically to work on it.

(15) Encouraging citizens to vote.

(16) Helping foreign-born people to secure naturalization papers.

(17) Helping provide places for living and working for displaced persons.

(18) Working for safety.

(19) Helping prevent forest fires; replanting under direction.

(20) Sending youth teams to needy small churches (under

159

supervision of denominational or interdenominational authorities).

The Group Members and Their Adult Workers Summarize the Results of Their Activities of Learning, in the Light of Their Purposes

Whether it be a Sunday church school class, an evening fellowship meeting, a committee responsibility or what, the experience of bringing together the various strands into summary should be regarded as a *necessary part of the process,* not something to do "after it is over." Provision for careful summary and evaluation should be allowed, in the time budget the groups make up at the beginning of the unit. They should expect to do unhurried bringing together of their findings, and looking at them in the light of the purposes with which they began. The time should allow for decision making, and possibly for some meaningful worship closing.

Evaluation should look for more than surface success. A worker may think, "Look! We have this interesting exhibit. We had a successful unit." Yes, from the angle of tangible products brought together, it may appear to have been successful. What about the inner experiences of the young people participating? Did they understand more fully, because of the activities? Were some confused ideas cleared up for them? Are their appreciations deepened and their sympathies broadened? The teacher may point to a blackboard full of points discussed. But did the young persons appear to have made these ideas their own? Did they reach conclusions which may be powerful enough and deep-felt enough to make a difference in daily living? Will they now approach persons of another background with finer sympathies? Are they more eager to live the Christlike way in the particular area of their lives that the unit has been about?

Youth know. They are the only ones who do. No adult can answer such questions for them. But a teacher asks, "How find time to evaluate when we have so little time in our classes or meetings as it is?" Two answers: (1) work for more time; (2) budget with the help of the young people themselves the time available. For to summarize and evaluate is a necessity, not a luxury in the learning

160

process. It is a live part that cannot be amputated without crippling the vital experience as a whole.

Questions such as the following may be considered by the young persons themselves:

What new thoughts have we gained that we did not have before? What former ideas have we expanded and stretched?

Was everyone interested? What were some evidences? What seemed to cause the interest (or the lack of it)? Did the interest hold up until the end? Why, or why not?

Did each one participate in some way? What were some of the ways?

Were we sure of our purposes when we started out? What were these purposes? Did we make our plans carefully? Wisely? Were our responsibilities faithfully carried out?

Was the Bible used? In what ways? How could it have been more fully or more fruitfully used? Did we in this unit learn more about the Bible? What are some of the evidences?

Did we reach helpful conclusions through this unit? What were they? Are these conclusions in harmony with the teachings of Jesus as we understand them?

Were we conscious of the presence of God as we worked and discussed? Were there any times of prayer?

Was there good group fellowship as we worked? Any difficulties in getting along with one another? If so, what were the causes and what was done about them?

Did we make any plans for service activities growing out of this unit? What will we need to do now, in carrying out those plans?

Are there any questions or problems still unsolved? When can they be faced? Has a record been made of them to remind us?

What suggestions do we have for ways we could improve our use of future units?

Are we better Christians because of our working and thinking and praying and serving together through this unit?

XIV

WAYS THE TEACHER GROWS

Not as though I had already attained, either were already perfect: but I follow after, if that I may apprehend that for which also I am of Christ Jesus. PHILIPPIANS 3:12

Somewhere in somebody's class or in some youth fellowship group, this very next Sunday will sit a young person facing a decision that will give his life an upward or a downward direction—irrevocably. Somewhere will sit some young person in whose fertile brain is forming a pattern for international dealings—but he needs a clearer understanding of the Christian ideal. Somewhere will sit the Lincolns, the Columbuses, the Mozarts, the Wattses, the Wesleys, the Einsteins, the Kagawas, or the public enemies. To paraphrase Winston Churchill's statement in terms of teachers of young people, never perhaps in the history of the Christian church has so much depended on so few.

In the quiet of his own heart, every parent, or Sunday school teacher or other worker with young people faces a crossroads. He could give up. "The work is too important, and I have so little time to give with all my other activities." He could say, "Find someone who is better prepared." Let him be reminded that when persons become humble enough, God can help them grow. And the church will stand by a teacher who wants to become a better one, with an abundance of aids.

But the crucial test, the test which should determine whether or not a worker will keep on with or take a new responsibility in working with young people, is the quality of his commitment. Here is the real crossroads. Will he keep on vaguely, living as a lukewarm Christian perhaps and giving stintingly of time and energy, with little concern for better methods or materials? Or will he launch forth bravely into a task he knows is too great for him, yet with ever-

162

growing consciousness of the limitless resources of an ever-creative
God?

> "There is only one miracle," said the Lord. "All else is
> cause and effect. All else is law."
> . . . "That miracle is the human soul."

. . . .

> "But," said the Lord—and the stars in the sky seemed
> to stand still and listen,
> "The power must be released, as the atom-breakers released
> the power of the atom."

. . . .

> "Perhaps," he said, "there's something in you."[1]

The Church Helps Its Workers Grow

Each church, small or large, has high stewardship to challenge all
its workers in home and church to seek to achieve their highest and
best: to grow in preparation for the sacred task of guiding young
lives; to grow in service. There are two kinds of workers. One, as he
looks back, will have had twenty years' experience. Another will
have had one year's experience repeated twenty times. Experience
alone is not enough. Practice may make perfect in wrong directions.
The church should challenge to one's heroic best, then offer resources and guidance.

Crucially determinative is the time of recruiting a new worker.
Do the church representatives use persuasive words, cloak over the
bigness of the task perhaps in eagerness to get a class manned,
minimize the demands as to preparation and training and time to be
spent with the young persons outside of the regular meetings? A
teacher excuses herself from attending a leadership education course
on the grounds that she was "overpersuaded" to take her class in the
first place. An adviser says that he made it clear to the church representatives when they were talking with him about meeting with an
evening group, that he had but little time to give. His complaints
were brushed off, as if working with young persons these days would
cost but little time! How could he be blamed for responding but on
lower levels of half commitment?

Church boards or committees of education should establish and maintain strict policies: qualifications for prospective workers, steps of training and preparation to be required. Suppose some worker be screened out? Would it not be better to let two classes be combined temporarily under a strong leader than to recruit hurriedly, over-persuade, and then find it difficult to unenlist later a teacher who is not giving his best?

In one small-to-medium church where formerly slipshod work was countenanced, standards were set up *by the workers themselves* and affirmed by the church board of education: statements of what they felt their young people, their church, and their God had the right to expect of them. Plans were made for finding and training prospective workers *ahead* of need, not waiting for an emergency situation where a class was without a teacher or a group of youth without an adviser. Gradually effort was made to set up a "double staff," with a lead teacher and associate (not mere substitute!) for each group. Now the pastor reports a *waiting list* of prospective workers. People need but to be challenged.

In another church, the college-age youth wanted to ask a brilliant young lawyer who had recently joined the church to work with them. His first response was "No!" And his tone of voice seemed to imply, "I cannot waste my time on inconsequential things." But when the church representative and delegation of young people made clear to him the vital work of that church school, and suggested a time of probation in which they would determine whether they felt he had the spiritual depth and skill in guiding their discussions adequately, he was humbled and impressed. "Sunday school must have changed since I grew up," he remarked. "It used to be just anybody could do it." He agreed to meet with these keen-minded, energetic young people during a specified period. He tried to rise to what they expected and eventually became a splendid teacher. His feet were started on the path of growth from the beginning!

A probationary period should be considered a "must." Where a church has a plan for training workers ahead, after attending a leadership class for a time, workers may assist lead teachers as resource helpers. Because materials for youth groups are in units, a

164

convenient plan would be for a prospective worker to assist during a certain unit; the young people and he become acquainted; he gets insight through fellowship with them. It may be that he will decide that he is not the one to work with that particular age level.

Even after tryout, no worker should ever be invited in any church to any post of service for more than a year at a time! Every worker for any age should be up for re-examination by church boards before staffs are made up for the ensuing year. There should be an installation service in a congregational worship period: a time when workers, parents, and others of the church body make high affirmation of new commitment, and link hands together in a task involving close co-operation at all times between home and church. When it is clear that installation is for a year at a time, the church officials are upheld in their standards and should not be embarrassed to suggest to one who is failing to achieve them that he be relieved. A worker who fails in regular attendance, preparation, or efforts at improvement actually dismisses himself.

But even more vital than achievement of standards is the worker's growing experience in the Christian faith. The church, in recruiting, should make the questions about a person's faith the pivotal ones. Yet sometimes church representatives, in desperation to find workers, take for granted that because a person is a church member he is sufficiently grounded in the faith and fail to probe or to challenge. Does this prospective worker have daily habits of prayer? Participate regularly in church worship? Is he one who serves others naturally and as an expression of his Christian love and concern? What are his central beliefs about the nature of God? About His Son? About the Bible? About church? About sin and redemption?

Answers to such questions *cannot be taken for granted,* if the church wants to surround young lives with influences winsome for the Christian way. Young people are acutely sensitive to personalities. They are uncompromising in their idealism, in what they expect of their teachers. One father of an intermediate girl and a senior boy was speaking of an attractive, popular teacher in their church school:

Her techniques are undoubtedly excellent. She works hard at the job. But it appears that she has little to give—I mean, no warm, glowing

165

religious experience, apparently. She uses vague terms about what she believes. If the young people ask questions about God or Jesus or the Bible, she seems at a loss. And you can't fool young people!

A teacher recounts her own story:

"How about taking over this class of intermediates that has been so long without a teacher?" my superintendent asked me one day. He explained that the ranks were low. Some had become too busy. Some had moved out of town. At first I failed to take the idea seriously. Ever since I could remember, the church had been needing teachers—especially teachers of intermediates! I had never thought of myself in that connection. What did I know about that age, or, for that matter, about teaching? What if I could not keep order? What if they asked me questions I couldn't answer? What if I wanted to go out of town some Sunday?

I suspected that I had been asked as a last resort. "I'm entirely too busy," I thought to myself. "I'm up to my ears in church work. Let someone else better qualified take over."

When the pastor and intermediate counselor came, however, I gave in—partially, I suppose, because I felt a bit sorry for them. "Well," I said, "I'll help you out for just a little while, until you can find somebody else." I expected them to look relieved; to congratulate me.

But instead they were troubled, and shook their heads. "No!" I was taken aback. "We cannot accept that kind of motive on your part. Don't take a class to help us out. Think of the boys and girls. Ask God to lead you. Then tell us what you decide."

I was beginning to feel frightened. I would tell them I was too busy. But something kept calling . . . insistent as the hound of heaven. Thoughts came to me in the night watches. "Your chance to build with God . . . to contribute something that will endure beyond your life . . . your stake in tomorrow's world . . ."

I took the class. And I took it humbly. Every time I meet with those wide-awake, responsive boys and girls I feel less sure of my own capabilities, but more thrilled at the privilege of being their teacher. I have now given up several other offices to allow for more time to prepare and to be with them outside of church hours. The rewards I have experienced are impossible to put into words. God was never so close to me as now since I have been working with these intermediates.

The Worker's Own Long-Range Plan for Growth

Each teacher of youth in the church, and every parent (who is preeminently a teacher) can set for himself some specific steps forward.

The church can provide for group meetings where parents and other teachers can meet in fellowship and minister to one another's growth: in their understanding of youth, in their beliefs and commitment, in their skills for conversing with youth about deeper questions of life.

Possibly each individual will wish to have some way of evaluating his progress forward. The adventurous teacher will ask himself such questions as the following from time to time:

1. *Am I growing religiously?*

Am I investing in spiritual growth—through worshiping in my church fellowship, through remembering daily to spend some time in meditation, Bible reading, and prayer, through striving to maintain, as nearly as I know how, a Christian point of view in all my relationships?

Am I achieving a degree of that "inner calm" that keeps me from losing poise and loving spirit in difficult situations? Can my youth see in me the workings of a religion strong enough to "hold" under strain, and secure enough to answer the restless of their lives?

This year . . . it might be well to think of "being calm." . . . Teachers are responsible for the atmosphere in which the world's future leaders are developing. If they can demonstrate how to relax and receive as well as they show their willingness to give, a great wave of co-operative thinking may eventually "calm" the world.[2]

Time may be set aside in workers' conference meetings at the church for discussion of ideas of God so that parents and teachers may strive together to help their young people develop richer, fuller ideas. They may tell one another about what worship means in their own lives, and worship practices in the family and at church; and they may seek ever better ways of guiding the awakening worship impulses of the young. Such meetings can be times of heart-searching and spiritual refreshment.

An important personal quest for each worker is that of creedmaking for himself: trying to put on paper clearly and accurately what he believes and why; trying to express in words in group discussion. All persons need practice putting convictions into words, that they may

167

more easily and naturally "speak a word for Christ" when the opportunity comes. At the nuclear center of every situation is a fluid mass, a point unhardened as yet; the proper thought brought at the strategic moment may be the deciding factor in starting the spiral upward instead of downward, for re-forming. As parents and workers with youth set themselves on spiritual quest, they will strive constantly and humbly to "live beyond themselves" each day, that they may be worthy companions of youth who must learn to live beyond where the teachers now are!

The workers and parents of one church[3] put their own creed into words. It is used in installations, and takes on ever more meaning as they move out spiritually upon its affirmations.

I am teaching youth because . . .

I believe in God and His purposes for mankind. I believe in the power of God that can come into young lives and transform them, and through them, society.

I believe in Jesus, and that the Way which He lived and taught can become the way of abundant living for all peoples, if the youth of tomorrow's world learn to practice it today.

I believe in the Bible, and that it has a message for youth today as in the ages past.

I believe in the Church, as a fellowship of working Christians who have an important job to do. I am thankful to have a share in its work.

I believe in the educational work of the church. I have faith in educational evangelism, in the possibility of bringing young persons to know God and of leading them into ever closer relationship with him.

I believe in Youth. I think of them as intelligent, and capable of sharing in God's purposes for them. I believe in the methods which will encourage them to develop their growing abilities, and which will offer them the best resources of the past and present—in the Bible, the Church, the resources of the Christian heritage, and the lives of Christian persons.

I believe in myself. I have faith that in spite of my weakness and faults, God can and will use me to do His work if I but give myself whole-heartedly for His cause. I will do my best to "attempt great things for God, expect great things from God."

2. *Am I growing in my understanding of young people, and especially of that age with which I am privileged to work?*

Am I growing in my belief in young persons? In my willingness
168

to trust them to the full extent of their powers? Do I rejoice in evidences of their growing maturity, even though this maturation robs me of chances to play as active a part in guiding them as formerly? Am I overcoming the temptation to respond emotionally when a young person refuses to co-operate with my plans or seems not to like me; and am I growing in open and permissive spirit so as to understand more clearly his motives?

Do I enjoy being with these young persons in activities during weekdays? Do I look forward with tingling zest to times I will spend with them, individually or as a group? Am I becoming better acquainted with their parents and their home backgrounds? Am I aware of other circles of relationships that are influencing their attitudes and actions?

Am I learning better how to adapt my own ratio of initiative and helpfulness to their ratio of abilities and readinesses? Am I reading books and conferring with others that can help me understand more clearly how to work with this particular age level? Do I know when help from me is needed, and when to withhold? When to speak and when to be silent? Am I alert to individual variations of growth?

Am I observing the fellowship level when my class or group meets together—the "ins," the "outs," the "fringers," the "isolates"? Are we moving gradually toward fuller, more cohesive fellowship and more spontaneous practices of friendliness? Are we reaching and warmly welcoming unreached ones?

Workers and parents may ask themselves if they are growing also in their understanding of themselves, their insights into promptings and interests that drive them? The understanding of young personalities involves opening one's heart to persons in general, their strivings and drivings, their weaknesses and wants. To paraphrase the greatest insight on human relationships ever given the world, "Love thy youth . . . as thyself."

Youth after all are *persons*. And adults who associate with youth in home and church are persons. Each might be surprised to know that the other has similar tensions, yearnings, dreams, griefs and secret hurts. Let the adult worker, then, chuckle a bit to himself as he goes out to understand youth better. He will find himself mirrored often. And the swift sympathy of youth, their unlimited idealism, and their buoyant adventurousness will catch him up in its swing. He will love them in their impracticality and they will respond instinctively to his understanding.[4]

3. *Am I growing in my understanding of the Bible, in my zest for continued Bible study, and in my personal exemplification of the Bible message in my daily living?*

Parents and other teachers will find it helpful for their own personal enrichment as well as for their preparation for guiding younger minds, to meet for study of the Bible and its message themselves. Courses are available, some through correspondence, through the leadership curricula of the denominations. Books will be recommended from denominational headquarters; references are often found listed in the teachers' and parents' helps in the youth curricula.

Careful individual or group reading of selected portions, as for example one gospel taken for extended study, imparts fresh insight and leads to further adventures. Use of different translations imparts glints of new light on half-understood passages. Films may be secured for group meetings of parents and other teachers.

Questions parents and teachers have about the "coverage" of Bible in the curriculum units offered intermediates, seniors, and young people can be answered through charts and explanatory literature available from denominational headquarters; oftentimes, a field worker can be secured through denominational offices to explain how the curriculum units are developed, the philosophy back of the approaches to the Bible involved, and methods of interpreting the Bible to young people.

Parents and teachers will do well to give their firsthand attention to the units as they appear for use with youth, taking time to look up the Bible references suggested and to think about their meanings—that they may be prepared to converse intelligently with the boys and girls. Teachers and parents may decide what books, maps, pictures, and other helps for Bible adventures may be purchased for the church library or passed around among the homes.

The helpfulness of pastors who have had training in Bible in seminaries and in their special courses of study, should be called upon. Through teaching the teachers of young people, pastors can often make a far greater and more influential investment of their time than merely by meeting occasionally with the young people themselves.

4. *Am I growing in my understanding of better methods, and in my skill and confidence for using them?*

"But suppose," one worker asks earnestly, "I *do* want to learn to be a better teacher. I can't seem to 'get the hang' of it. Something seems to block me from trying new ideas, like 'activities' I find suggested in the teachers' helps. Perhaps I am afraid the young people will get 'out of hand,' or that 'discipline' problems will develop. I feel more secure in the old familiar pattern of reading the Scripture verses around and asking questions." Here is a worker with a glimmering of good intentions, perhaps limited experience with only one pattern of teaching, and honesty in facing his problem. A few home-spun suggestions may help him in his *attitudes;* his church with leadership courses, books, helpful counsel, and other aids is ready to help him practically.

a. *Let the hesitant teacher remember that every good teacher had to have a first time for trying a new method.* Maybe he did not experience success with the first try, but he kept on. Security in newer and better ways grows through experience, just as one's present securities in older and perhaps poorer methods grew through experience.

b. *Let a worker experiment with activity suggestions from the teacher's helps by himself first.* He may be tempted to discount, or even skip suggestions from the writers that the youth be given a chance to choose and use "activities" of various kinds. One worker found a suggestion for blueprints and carbon prints of leaf patterns as a means whereby the boys and girls may be led to fuller reverential awareness of design and order in God's plan. This teacher decided that if the writer could make such prints, she would try. One afternoon when her family was away, she secured the materials suggested and followed the directions (much as if she were baking a cake)

171

until—proud as any intermediate herself—she exhibited her creative handiwork to an amazed family. "Now if my class gets half as much fun out of it as I did . . ."

c. *Let helpful resource persons in specialized fields be invited to assist with certain units or with particular activities.* Sometimes workers are willing to venture into new activities of learning involving constructon or making records or other work with paper, but shy away from more complicated methods such as role playing or other variations of impromptu dramatization. Perhaps in the church or community there will be a person not now serving in the church who has talent or training along these lines. He may be delighted to help. Contact with different personalities can be enriching to the young people; and experiences in varied lines may help ferret out a buried talent and potential vocational or hobby interest!

A senior group, moved by powerful scenes they were discovering in the Amos story, invited a drama major from a nearby college to assist them in writing script and filming their dramatization.

The regular teacher or counselor himself does not need to possess all the skills for all possible activities of learning. Sometimes in his class or group will be young persons who themselves can take over. This happened in a situation where with a Bible unit a suggestion was found for choral reading. The first impulse of the teacher was to omit that idea. But he decided to mention it as a possibility, and immediately several members of the group who (unknown before to the teacher) were in a choral group in their high school, took over the responsibility of preparing a psalm for reading chorally in a worship service.

Where assistant resource helpers are called in, the regular teacher or counselor himself remains on the job providing continuity, and helping the group keep a clear sense of purpose through the activity.

d. *Let a growing teacher start with his own strongest point.* Self-understanding, of one's strengths as well as of one's weaknesses, is important for any worker. From standing squarely and confidently in a method he can surely use, a worker may venture one step into a less familiar method. Only one step need be taken at a time.

e. *Let a goal be set for the next few weeks, as to some particular*
172

method in which a worker wishes to grow. One teacher recognized his weakness in periods of discussion. Youth response was lacking. "They shut up like clams." He began working on that method. He ordered helps from his denominational headquarters and from the United States Department of Agriculture.[5] He discovered the variations of discussion such as panel, Socratic dialogue, "buzz-groups." He learned the importance of using discussion topics clear enough and simple enough (and with varying potential viewpoints) so that his young people could get hold of them, and share from their experiences or thoughts. He found that facts are often needed, and learned that activities of research may be correlated with discussion. He concluded that he had expected sharing sometimes when his young people did not have adequate background to be able to decide what their viewpoints were.

He tried to phrase lead questions more clearly and pointedly, so as to offer the young people a handle, whereas formerly he had left them "up in the air" as vague generalizations. What is more, he began practicing on his good friends, testing himself in stimulating discussion and in watching its course toward a conclusion. In a surprisingly short time, he noticed a "perking up" of interest in his class. As his own abilities and confidence grew, the responses of his young people warmed and became more free and spontaneous. He was no longer afraid of this . . . or of the *next* method. Now more relaxed, both he and his group could pursue more naturally and freely their thinking and planning, until methods became "almost unconscious" as means to larger ends. As with the little engine pulling up the hill, the "I-think-I-can-attitude" is the one that wins.

f. *Let the worker avoid excusing failure by blaming circumstances that might, at least to an extent, be controlled, or bettered.*

One of the most serious difficulties in the way of teacher growth is the attitude (often unconscious) of looking for excuses. "Suggestions such as these I find in the teachers' helps sound as if they are meant for college-trained people. Look at me—I didn't even get to finish high school." "That might work in a *big* church but surely it is not meant for a small one like mine."

One needs, for venturing out upon better methods of working with

173

young people, not necessarily a college education but an open mind and committed heart, trust in young persons and in the learning process. And workers in small and medium churches might be surprised were they able to see as if through television the writers of such lesson helps as those about which they complain, accomplishing just such results as they tell about under difficult conditions oftentimes in the smaller and less well-equipped churches. There are ways of overcoming, or of making the best of, adverse physical circumstances. The key is in the attitude of the worker.

g. *Let the worker remember that common sense, a bit of humor, and the genial good spirit of young people themselves will carry through difficult situations.* Old mistakes can be left behind. Common sense will light the way for the next step ahead. Not *all* better methods need be attempted at once. The Chinese have a saying that "a journey of a thousand miles begins with a single step." The worker can take the immediate step that good sense suggests. He is not expected to duplicate exactly what some other teacher has done. Rather, let him find with his own young people the best ways of working problems through together. Their appreciation and response will in turn create momentum for the next adventure forward.

The Master Teacher Leads the Way

Beyond all the helpful discoveries as to methods, psychology, Bible research and the like, the Great Teacher is yonder ahead. No "techniques" have ever been found that surpassed those He used. Yet He used good methods so naturally that one must look twice to discover, through the very warmth and understanding of His human contacts, what His ways were. Thus it is with a good teacher. He seeks ever to apprehend better ways of understanding and guiding young persons in their upward growth; yet ever is the method suffused with warmth and glow of loving concern from the heart.

Anyone working with young persons today would do well to reread the Four Gospels, visualizing Jesus the Teacher, tracing methods He used through insights offered by modern psychology and educational research. Watch Him as He went about loving people, warming their awakening aspirations by His genuine appreciation of their

174

real selves and their secret dreams, probing the subsoils of their motives. Then, by His expectation of their best response, and His utter trust in the power of God working in and through them, we see Him calling forth a nobility of purpose and a vastness of strength they themselves did not know was theirs! "Techniques" would be too poor a word for such a process.

Yet in essence that is just what it means to be a teacher and counselor of young persons today. Here are no elaborate devices to manipulate response, no contests, no testing as to facts learned or verses memorized, no artificial awards, no impatience to cover lessons. A few homespun stories, a few pictures of persons in action . . . but *always* an ushering of the individual into the presence of the Father. Extensive equipment He surely did not have. But He could pick a flower by the wayside and tell a story in such a way as to leave meanings unmistakable for those who had "ears to hear."

Perhaps then, if we follow the Great Teacher, we discover that good teaching means chipping away nonessentials, even as "sculpturing" means releasing the image hidden in the marble.

For Jesus' methods, and all good teaching methods, *release* personality: from prejudices and institutionalism into freer channels for communion with the Father; from blindness into vision; from lameness into strength; from slavery to outworn concepts into wide horizons of understanding; from tensions and hatreds into good companionship; from lethargy into enthusiasm; from dead aspirations into life!

We are His apprentices, we who would guide His youth in a day like this. May our lives be released through His power into fuller service; and may our methods be such as to enable His spirit to release the lives of these now young into power and love to bless the world.

NOTES

[1] Frontispiece. P. R. Hayward, *The Dream of Power of Youth* (New York: Harper & Brothers, 1930), p. xiii. Reprinted with permission.

I. TEEN YEARS TODAY

1 Title of a study of youth and these times, National Education Association, 1952.

2 Goodwin Watson, *Youth After Conflict* (New York: Association Press, 1947).

3 From *Emotions and How They Grow*, by Virginia M. Axline. Reprinted from *Childhood Education*, Vol. 27, Nov., 1950 (Washington: A.C.E.I.).

4 R. J. Havighurst and Hilda Taba, *Adolescent Character and Personality* (New York: John Wiley and Sons, Inc., 1950).

5 Rowena Ferguson, *Teen Agers—Their Days and Ways* (Chicago: National Council of the Churches of Christ in the U.S.A., 1952), p. 28.

6 W. N. Pittenger, *The Historic Faith and a Changing World* (New York: Oxford University Press, 1950), p. 39.

7 Georgia Harkness, *The Modern Rival of the Christian Faith* (New York and Nashville: Abingdon-Cokesbury Press, 1952), p. 11.

8 *Ibid.*

9 *Op. cit.*, p. 16.

10 *Op. cit.*, p. 17.

II. CHRISTIAN AFFIRMATIONS AND YOUTH WORK

1 Matt. 22:37-40.

2 St. Augustine, Confessions I, 1.

3 See C. M. Bowman, *Restoring Worship* (New York and Nashville: Abingdon-Cokesbury Press, 1951) for suggestions for guiding children, youth and adults in ways of worship.

4 See *At Worship: Hymnal for Young Churchmen* (New York: Harper & Brothers, 1951), and recommended denominational hymnals.

5 Phrase of Dr. A. J. Gossip.

6 See Sabra Holbrook, *Children Object!* (New York: Viking Press, 1943).

7 Phrase of Rev. Harold Bremer.

8 P. R. Hayward, in *International Journal of Religious Education,*

176

May, 1929 (Chicago: Division of Christian Education, National Council of the Churches of Christ in the U.S.A.).

III. LONG-RANGE PLANNING IN THE CHURCH

1 See E. M. Conover, *The Church Builder,* and E. M. Conover, *The Church School and Parish House Building* (New York: The National Council of the Churches of Christ in the U.S.A., 1949).

IV. FELLOWSHIP: YOUTH WITH THEIR WORKERS

1 P. R. Hayward in *International Journal of Religious Education,* June, 1934 (Chicago: Division of Christian Education of the N.C.C.U.S.A.).
2 A. B. Hollingshead, *Elmtown's Youth* (New York: John Wiley and Sons, 1949).
3 Phrase of Miss Lucile Desjardins.
4 See N. J. Elliott, "Pattern of Friends in the Classroom," *Progressive Education,* Vol. 18, Nov., 1941, pp. 383-90; W. C. Olson, "The Improvement of Human Relations in the Classroom," *Childhood Education,* Vol. 22, March, 1946, pp. 317-25. See also J. L. Moreno, *Who Shall Survive?* (Washington: Nervous and Mental Disease Publishing Company, 1934).
5 United Christian Youth Movement, Division of Christian Education, National Council of the Churches of Christ in the U.S.A., Chicago, Ill.

V. WAYS YOUTH LEARN

1 W. H. Kilpatrick, "The Role of Camping in Education," in *The Camping Magazine,* Feb., 1942. See also Sixth Yearbook, John Dewey Society, p. 199.
2 G. W. Allport, *The Individual and His Religion* (New York: The Macmillan Company, 1950), pp. 41-42.

VI. SOME TYPES OF UNITS FOR LEARNING

1 Kilpatrick, *op. cit.*

XI. YOUTH LEARNING THROUGH WORSHIP

1 Adapted from Howard Brinton, *Quaker Education in Theory and Practice* (Pendle Hill Pamphlet Number 9 [Revised], 1949).

XIV. WAYS THE TEACHER GROWS

1 Hermann Hagedorn, *The Bomb That Fell on America* (New York: Association Press, 1948).

2 *Journal of Teacher Education* of Nebraska, Vol. 23 (1943), p. 245.

3 Workers of Winfield Methodist Church, Little Rock, Ark., Mrs. C. B. Nelson.

4 Suggested by D. A. Thom, *Normal Youth and Its Everyday Problems* (New York: Appleton-Century-Crofts, 1924), pp. 151, 246.

5 Guidance materials for discussion group leaders and for discussion group members, United States Department of Agriculture, Washington, D.C.

BIBLIOGRAPHY

ON THE CHRISTIAN FAITH AND PHILOSOPHY
OF EDUCATION

ALLPORT, G. W. *The Individual and His Religion: A Psychological Interpretation.* New York: The Macmillan Company, 1950.

AMERICAN COUNCIL ON EDUCATION. *Emotion and the Educative Process.* Washington: American Council on Education, 1938.

At Worship: Hymnal for Young Churchmen. New York: Harper & Brothers, 1951.

AUBREY, E. E. *Present Theological Tendencies.* New York: Harper & Brothers, 1936.

BAILLIE, JOHN. *A Diary of Private Prayer.* New York: Charles Scribner's Sons, 1940.

BEAVER, G. A. *Christ and Community.* New York: Association Press, 1950.

BOWMAN, C. M. *Restoring Worship.* New York and Nashville: Abingdon-Cokesbury Press, 1951.

BRAMELD, T. B. H. *Ends and Means in Education: A Midcentury Appraisal.* New York: Harper & Brothers, 1950.

BROWNELL, BAKER. *The Human Community.* New York: Harper & Brothers, 1950.

BUSHNELL, HORACE. *Christian Nurture* (rev. L. A. Weigle). New York: Charles Scribner's Sons, 1916.

BUTTS, R. F. *The American Tradition in Religion and Education.* Boston: The Beacon Press, 1950.

BUTTRICK, G. A. *Faith and Education.* New York and Nashville: Abingdon-Cokesbury Press, 1952.

CANTRIL, HADLEY. *The "Why" of Man's Experience.* New York: The Macmillan Company, 1950.

CARRIER, BLANCHE. *Free to Grow.* New York: Harper & Brothers, 1951.

CASWELL, HOLLIS L. (ED.). *The American High School: Its Responsibility and Opportunity.* New York: Harper & Brothers, 1947.

CHAVE, E. J. *A Functional Approach to Religious Education.* Chicago: University of Chicago Press, 1931.

CHILDS, J. L. *Education and Morals: An Experimentalist Philosophy of Education.* New York: Appleton-Century-Crofts, 1950.

DEWOLF, L. H. *The Religious Revolt Against Reason.* New York: Harper & Brothers, 1949.

DeWolf, L. H. "Theology Needed at Toronto," in *The Christian Century*, April 5, 1950.

Elliott, H. S. *Can Religious Education Be Christian?* New York: The Macmillan Company, 1947.

A Guide to True Peace. New York: Harper & Brothers, 1950.

Harkness, Georgia. *Understanding the Christian Faith*. New York and Nashville: Abingdon-Cokesbury Press, 1947.

————. *The Modern Rival of the Christian Faith*. New York and Nashville: Abingdon-Cokesbury Press, 1952.

Harner, N. C. *I Believe*. Philadelphia: Christian Education Press, 1950.

Kelley, E. C. *Education for What Is Real*. New York: Harper & Brothers, 1947.

Kelly, Thomas. *A Testament of Devotion*. New York: Harper & Brothers, 1941.

Lewis, H. D. *Morals and the New Theology*. New York: Harper & Brothers, 1948.

Livingstone, Sir Richard. *Education for a World Adrift*. New York: The Macmillan Company, 1944.

————. *The Future in Education*. New York: The Macmillan Company, 1944.

Lotz, P. H. (ed.). *Orientation in Religious Education*. New York and Nashville: Abingdon-Cokesbury Press, 1950.

Marrow, A. J. *Living without Hate: Scientific Approaches to Human Relations*. New York: Harper & Brothers, 1952.

McKibben, F. M. *Christian Education Through the Church*. New York and Nashville: Abingdon-Cokesbury Press, 1947.

Mead, Margaret. *The School in American Culture*. Cambridge: Harvard University Press, 1951.

Miller, R. C. *The Clue to Christian Education*. New York: Charles Scribner's Sons, 1950.

Nash, Arnold (ed.). *Protestant Thought in the Twentieth Century: Whence and Whither?* New York: The Macmillan Company, 1951.

Piaget, Jean. *The Moral Judgment of the Child*. London: Routledge & Kegan Paul, Ltd., 1932.

Plant, J. S. *Personality and the Cultural Pattern*. New York: The Commonwealth Fund, 1937.

Radcliffe, L. J. *Making Prayer Real*. New York and Nashville: Abingdon-Cokesbury Press, 1952.

Read, Herbert. *Education Through Art*. First Published and all rights: Faber and Faber, London, 2nd ed., 1945.

Ross, Murray. *The Religious Beliefs of Youth*. New York: Association Press, 1950.

SEIFERT, HARVEY. *Fellowships of Concern*. New York and Nashville: Abingdon-Cokesbury Press, 1949.

UNDERHILL, EVELYN. *Worship*. New York: Harper & Brothers, 1937.

VAN DUSEN, H. P. *God in Education*. New York: Charles Scribner's Sons, 1951.

ON METHODS OF WORKING WITH YOUNG PEOPLE

ASSOCIATION FOR SUPERVISION AND CURRICULUM DEVELOPMENT. *Towards Better Teaching*. Washington: National Education Association, 1949 (Yearbook).

BARR, A. S., BURTON, W. H., AND BRUECKNER, L. I. *Supervision*. New York: Appleton-Century-Crofts, 1947.

BARZUN, JACQUES. *Teacher in America*. Boston: Little, Brown & Co., 1945.

BAXTER, BERNICE, AND CASSIDY, ROSALIND. *Group Experience—The Democratic Way*. New York: Harper & Brothers, 1943.

BLUMENTHAL, L. H. *Administration of Group Work*. New York: Association Press, 1948.

BOWMAN, C. M. *Guiding Intermediates*. New York and Nashville: Abingdon-Cokesbury Press, 1943.

BROWN, SPENCER. *They See for Themselves*. New York: Harper & Brothers, 1945.

CARLSON, R. E. *Nature Lore Manual for Church Leaders*. New York and Nashville: Abingdon-Cokesbury Press, 1948.

CHAPLIN, DORA. *Children and Religion*. New York: Charles Scribner's Sons, 1948.

COBER, K. L., AND STRICKER, E. *Teaching Seniors*. Philadelphia: Judson Press, 1940.

COYLE, G. L. *Group Work with American Youth*. New York: Harper & Brothers, 1948.

―――. *Group Experience and Democratic Values*. New York: Woman's Press, 1948.

CUTTON, J. M. *Teaching Young People*. Philadelphia: Judson Press, 1941.

DALE, EDGAR. *Audio-Visual Methods in Teaching*. New York: Dryden Press, 1945.

DESJARDINS, LUCILE. *Teaching Intermediates*. Philadelphia: Judson Press.

DIMOCK, H. S., AND HENDRY, C. E. *Camping and Character*. New York: Association Press, 1929.

DIMOCK, H. S., AND TRECKER, H. B. *Supervision of Group Work and Recreation*. New York: Association Press, 1949.

181

EAKIN, MILDRED AND FRANK. *The Church School Teacher's Job*. New York: The Macmillan Company, 1949.

EAVEY, C. B. *Principles of Personality Building for Christian Parents.* Grand Rapids: Zondervan Press, 1952.

EDUCATIONAL POLICIES COMMISSION. *Moral and Spiritual Values in the Public Schools*. Washington: National Education Association, 1951.

EHRENSPERGER, H. A. *Conscience on Stage*. New York and Nashville: Abingdon-Cokesbury Press, 1947.

EISENBERG, H. AND L. *The Pleasure Chest*. Nashville: The Parthenon Press, 1949.

ELLIOTT, H. S. *The Process of Group Thinking*. New York: Association Press, 1938.

GRIFFITHS, L. B. *Missionary Education for the Junior High School Age*. New York: Friendship Press, 1948.

HARNER, N. C. *Youth Work in the Church*. New York and Nashville: Abingdon-Cokesbury Press, 1942.

HARTMAN, GERTRUDE. *Finding Wisdom*. New York: The John Day Co., 1938.

HELSETH, I. O. *Living in the Classroom*. Ann Arbor: Edward Press, Inc., 1939.

HIGHET, GILBERT. *The Art of Teaching*. New York: A. A. Knopf, 1950.

JERSILD ET AL. *Child Development and the Curriculum*. New York: Columbia University Press, 1946.

KILPATRICK, W. H. *Modern Education and Better Human Relations* (Freedom Pamphlets). New York: Anti-Defamation League of B'nai B'rith, 1951.

KILPATRICK, W. H., AND VAN TIL, W. (EDS.). *Intercultural Attitudes in the Making*. New York: Harper & Brothers, 1947.

LAUBACH, F. C. *Teaching the World to Read*. New York: Friendship Press, 1947.

LEWIN, KURT. "Group Decision and Social Change," in *Readings in Social Psychology*. New York: Harper & Brothers, 1947.

————. *Resolving Social Conflicts*. New York: Harper & Brothers, 1947.

LEWIN, KURT, LIPPITT, R., AND ESCALONA, S. K. *Studies in Topological and Vector Psychology, I*. Ames, Iowa: University of Iowa Studies in Child Welfare, 1940, XVI, No. 3.

LINDHORST, F. A. *The Minister Teaches Religion*. New York and Nashville: Abingdon-Cokesbury Press, 1945.

LIPPITT, RONALD. *Training in Community Relations: A Research Exploration Toward New Group Skills* (Publication of the Research Center for Group Dynamics of the University of Michigan and the Commission on Community Interrelations of the American Jewish Congress). New York: Harper & Brothers, 1949.

May, Rollo. *The Art of Counseling*. New York and Nashville: Abingdon-Cokesbury Press, 1939.

McLester, F. C. *Teaching in the Church School*. New York and Nashville: Abingdon-Cokesbury Press, 1940.

―――. *What Is Teaching?* New York and Nashville: Abingdon-Cokesbury Press, 1934.

McRae, Glenn. *Teaching Youth in the Church*. St. Louis: Christian Board of Publication, 1940.

Moon, Alleen. *The Christian Education of Older Youth*. New York and Nashville: Abingdon-Cokesbury Press, 1943.

Moseley, F. A. and J. E. *Using Drama in the Church*. St. Louis: Christian Board of Publication, 1939.

Niebuhr, Hulda. *Ventures in Dramatics with Boys and Girls of the Church School*. New York: Charles Scribner's Sons, 1935.

Noel, E. G., and Leonard, J. P. *Foundations for Teacher Education in Audio-Visual Instruction*. Washington: American Council on Education, 1947.

Ott, Elmer. *So You Want to Be a Camp Counselor*. New York: Association Press, 1946.

Ownbey, R. L. *Evangelism in Christian Education*. New York and Nashville: Abingdon-Cokesbury Press.

Payne, E. C. "Moses Is Nobody," in *The Christian Century*, Jan. 24, 1951.

Price, Betty. *Adventuring in Nature*. New York: Association Press, 1940.

Rice, Rebecca. *Creative Activities*. Boston: Pilgrim Press, 1947.

Rich, Mark, et al. *Youth Work in the Rural Church*. St. Louis: Christian Board of Publication, 1940.

Shoemaker, S. S. *How You Can Help Other People*. New York: E. P. Dutton Co., 1946.

Sheviakov, A., and G. V., and Redl, Fritz. *Discipline for Today's Children and Youth*. Department of Supervision and Curriculum Development. Washington: National Educational Association, 1947.

Sherif, Muzafer. "Group Influences upon the Formation of Norms and Attitudes," in *The Psychology of Social Norms*. New York: Harper & Brothers, 1936.

Slavson, S. R. *Creative Group Education*. New York: Association Press, 1940.

―――. *Character Education in a Democracy*. New York: Association Press, 1939.

Stevens, Bertha. *Child and Universe*. New York: John Day and Co., 1931.

Tower, H. E. *Church Use of Audio-Visuals*. New York and Nashville: Abingdon-Cokesbury Press, 1951.

Utterback, W. E. *Decision Through Discussion*. Rev. ed. New York: Rinehart and Co., 1948.

Wilson, Gertrude, and Ryland, Gladys. *Social Group Work Practice*. Boston: Houghton-Mifflin, 1949.

Wittenberg, R. M. *So You Want to Help People*. New York: Association Press, 1947.

———. *The Art of Group Discipline*. New York: Association Press, 1951.

ON UNDERSTANDING YOUTH AND ACHIEVING FELLOWSHIP WITH THEM

Applegate, M. S. *Helping Boys in Trouble*. New York: Association Press, 1950.

Banay, R. S. *Youth in Despair*. New York: Coward-McCann, Inc., 1948.

Baruch, D. W. *New Ways in Discipline*. New York: McGraw-Hill Co., 1949.

Bertocci, P. A. *The Human Venture in Sex, Love, and Marriage*. New York: Association Press, 1949.

Blos, Peter. *The Adolescent Personality*. New York: Appleton-Century-Crofts, 1941.

Cole, Luella. *Psychology of Adolescence*. New York: Rinehart & Co., Inc., 1928.

Crawford, J. E., and Woodward, L. E. *Better Ways of Growing Up*. Philadelphia: Muhlenberg Press, 1948.

Crawford, John and Dorothea. *Teens: How to Solve Your Problems*. New York: Woman's Press, 1951.

Crow, L. D. and A. V. *Our Teen-Age Boys and Girls*. New York: McGraw-Hill Co., 1946.

Dahlberg, E. T. *Youth and the Homes of Tomorrow*. Philadelphia: Judson Press, 1934.

Daly, Maureen (ed.). *Profile of Youth* (by Members of the Staff of *The Ladies' Home Journal*). Philadelphia: J. B. Lippincott Co., 1952.

Dickerson, Roy. *Understanding Myself*. New York: Association Press, 1942.

Duvall, E. R. M. *Facts of Life and Love*. New York: Association Press, 1940.

———. *Keeping Up with the Teen-Agers*. Washington: Public Affairs Pamphlets, No. 127, 1947.

Duvall, E. R. M., and Hill, R. L. *When You Marry*. New York: Association Press, 1945.

184

DUVALL, S. M. *Before You Marry*. New York: Association Press, 1949.

FERGUSON, ROWENA. *Teen Agers—Their Days and Ways*. Chicago: National Council of the Churches of Christ in the U.S.A., 1952.

GRUENBERG, S. M. (ED.). *Our Children Today*. New York: Viking Press, 1952.

HARNER, N. C. *About Myself*. Philadelphia: Christian Education Press, 1950.

HAVIGHURST, R. J., AND TABA, HILDA. *Adolescent Character and Personality* (in collaboration with Andrew Brown and others. The Committee on Human Development of the University of Chicago). New York: John Wiley and Sons, 1949.

HAYWARD, P. R. *This Business of Living*. New York: Association Press, 1949.

HOLLINGWORTH, L. S. *The Psychology of the Adolescent*. New York: Appleton-Century-Crofts, 1928.

HOLLINGSHEAD, A. B. *Elmtown's Youth*. New York: John Wiley and Sons, 1949.

HORNEY, KAREN. *Our Inner Conflicts*. New York: W. W. Norton & Co., 1945.

JOHNSON, RANDOLPH, ET AL. *Looking Toward Marriage*. Boston: Allyn and Bacon, 1943.

KUNKEL, FRITZ. *What It Means to Grow Up*. New York: Charles Scribner's Sons, 1939.

———. *My Dear Ego*. Boston: Pilgrim Press, 1948.

LAWTON, GEORGE. *How to Be Happy Though Young*. New York: Vanguard Press, 1949.

MENNINGER, W. C. *Understanding Yourself*. Chicago: Science Research Associates, 1948.

MERRY, FRIEDA K. AND RALPH V. *The First Two Decades of Life*. New York: Harper & Brothers, 1950.

MURPHY, GARDNER. *Personality—A Biosocial Approach to Origins and Structures*. New York: Harper & Brothers, 1947.

NATIONAL ASSOCIATION OF SECONDARY SCHOOL PRINCIPALS. *Education for All American Youth*. Washington: National Education Association, 1944.

NELSON, J. O. *Young Laymen—Young Church*. New York: Association Press, 1948.

NEWCOMB, T. M., AND HARTLEY, E. L. *Readings in Social Psychology*. New York: Henry Holt & Co., 1947.

OVERTON, G. S. *Living with Teeners*. Nashville: Baptist Sunday School Board, 1950.

PEMBERTON, LOIS. *The Stork Didn't Bring You*. New York: H. K., 1948.

REMMERS, HERMAN H., AND HACKETT, C. G. *Let's Listen to Youth!* Chicago: Science Research Associates, 1950.

SHACTER, H. S. *Understanding Ourselves.* Bloomington, Ill.: McKnight and McKnight, 1945.

———. *How Personalities Grow.* Bloomington, Ill.: McKnight and McKnight, 1950.

STRAIN, F. B. *New Patterns in Sex Teaching.* New York: Appleton-Century-Crofts, 1934.

TAYLOR, F. M. *Their Rightful Heritage.* Boston: Pilgrim Press, 1942.

THOM, D. A. (M.D.). *Guiding the Adolescent.* Washington: United States Department of Labor, 1933.

INDEX

187